Textile Handbook

FIFTH EDITION

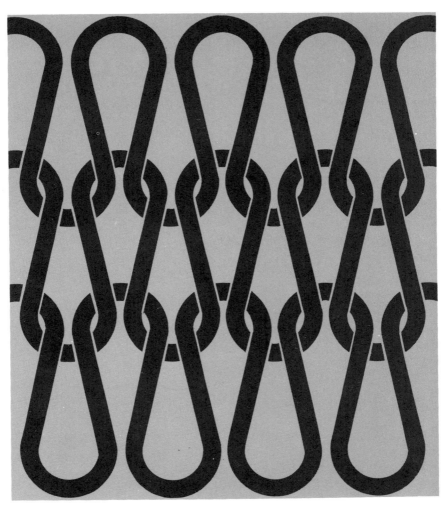

PUBLISHED BY THE AMERICAN HOME ECONOMICS ASSOCIATION
2010 MASSACHUSETTS AVENUE, N.W. • WASHINGTON, D.C. 20036

Library of Congress Cataloging in Publication Data

American Home Economics Association. Textiles and Clothing Section
Textile handbook

Bibliography: p.
Includes index
1. Textile industry and fabrics. I. Title.
TS1445.A46 1974   677'.002'02   74-31289

ISBN 0-8461-1611-1

Contents

Preface to Fifth Edition

Modern technology continues to change the characteristics and classifications of fibers and fabrics. During the short time that this revision was in process, two new generic classifications of fibers became known through their approval by the Federal Trade Commission (FTC). Man-made fibers now comprise about 50 percent of the fiber market. Within another 10 years, the synthetic fibers may hold as much as 80 percent of the market. Obviously, to produce a completely up-to-date revision of a textile handbook at any one time is about impossible.

However, this edition includes new information on fibers and yarns and their producers, on fabric finishes and dyes, on recent textile legislation and FTC regulations.

The Appendix and Bibliography have been revised to provide viable sources of current information. Throughout, of course, the basic facts that do not change remain the same.

Members of the revision committee who worked diligently to make this revision possible are: Janet Bubl, Ruth Galbraith, Pauline Jarma, Marjory Joseph, Sr. Ann Gabriel Kilsdonk, Mary Lapitsky, Rose Padgett, Delilah Roch, Wayne St. John, Teresa Wages, Jessie Warden, and Mary Jean Wylie. To all, sincere appreciation.

NORMA WALKER
Chairman, 1973-74 Revision Committee
AHEA Textiles and Clothing Section

Preface to Fourth Edition

In the decade since the American Home Economics Association first copyrighted the *Textile Handbook*, the textile industry has consistently grown and changed. Within the last year the Federal Trade Commission identified a new generic group of man-made fibers recently developed. Numbers of improved fabric finishes appeared—all intended to make life simpler and safer for the homemaker by protecting her family's clothing against shrinkage, wrinkles, soil, bacteria, flammability, and weather. Laws that govern the labeling of furs and fabrics were amended in a further effort to aid both industry and the confused shopper who finds herself confronted with bewildering abundance. The search for fast and easy means to care for clothing produced an array of new soaps and detergents. Facts about these separate yet essentially related subjects are contained in this latest edition of the handbook.

The tried-and-true information of the earlier editions still remains. Much of it will be new to the students and young homemakers who are only now discovering a need for this knowledge.

Among those who contributed their expertise toward the success of this booklet are Lois Dickey, Helen Gray, Alice Linn, Anne Lyng, Iola Mathias, Sue Morton, Dorothy Sparling, A. Frank Tesi, William Weaver, Rose White, and Maynette Williams. To them the chairman of the revisions committee is particularly grateful.

MAMIE HARDY
Chairman, 1969-70 Revision Committee
AHEA Textiles and Clothing Section

Introduction

Textiles today offer the consumer unending horizons of beauty, variety, and serviceability.

New developments constantly challenge the consumer to know his own needs and his own resources, to encourage the best efforts of industry, and to make wise, thoughtful choices.

Along with the beauty of textiles for clothing and environment, suitability and serviceability must also concern the consumer. These are the attributes with which this handbook is largely concerned.

Many individual properties combine to influence the manner in which a fabric or garment or household item performs in wear and in cleaning. The major ones are:

Fiber Content

A fabric composed 100 percent of any one given fiber may be expected to have different qualities than a fabric of one or more fibers blended together or in combination. For example: The qualities of a 100 percent silk fabric would be different from a fabric of 20 percent silk and 80 percent wool.

Yarn Construction

Fabrics may be made from any of the following yarns: filament or staple; woolen or worsted; carded or combed; relatively simple; complex novelty types; or textured yarns. Each type of yarn construction contributes certain qualities to a fabric.

Fabric Construction

Fabric construction may be simple or complex. There are a variety of standard weaves, knits, and other methods of fabrication that have become familiar over the years. But every year, the ingenious fabric designer may produce new and attractive fabric constructions.

Dyeing or Printing

Dyeing or printing of a fabric provides a wide selection of colors and designs. Dye chemistry and the proper application of dyes to fabrics play an important part in the satisfaction users receive from colored fabrics.

Finish

Many different physical and chemical finishes are applied to fabrics to give them added and desirable properties. They may also influence the use and care of fabrics.

Decorative Designs

Decorative designs may be applied to a fabric surface or as a part of the basic weave in construction. They add interest and variety. Many designs give very satisfactory performance in wear and in cleaning; some designs may limit the wear life of a fabric.

Garment Construction

The manner in which fabrics are combined in garment design and construction is a very important consideration for consumer satisfaction. In addition to a well-selected fabric, a garment must have proper cutting and good sewing if it is to be satisfactory in use.

Garment Findings and Trim

Findings and trim are as important as the fabric itself in garment design. If the stitching thread shrinks or interlining bleeds, if the bias or stay tape and the ribbon or embroidery trim do not perform satisfactorily in cleaning, much or all of the value of the garment is lost.

Fabric properties can be determined by laboratory tests, and often test results are used to prepare the labels, hang tags, and advertising and promotional material on textile merchandise. These are important sources of current information for the consumer.

Today the consumer's acquaintance with the world of textiles from fiber to finished product is a necessity as well as a pleasure. The information in this handbook has been chosen for its value in furthering a profitable acquaintance with today's textiles and for its usefulness in helping the consumer expand his knowledge in the future.

Chemical and Physical Properties of Textile Fibers

All textile fibers have certain physical and chemical properties that make them suitable for use in yarns and fabrics. These fiber properties carry over, in varying degrees, to yarn and fabric. Infinite research, experimentation, and skill have been, and still are being, devoted to studying, manipulating, and supplementing the properties of fibers to achieve desired results in yarn, fabric, and clothing. These efforts may extend even to the creation of certain properties or to the elimination of undesirable characteristics.

A chart on page 4 shows comparative values for some of the chemical and physical properties of fibers; other properties, such as affinity for dyes, resistance to light, and heat sensitivity, are discussed elsewhere.

Specific Gravity

The relative densities of textile fibers may be compared by means of specific gravity values, i.e., the ratio of the mass of material to the mass of an equal volume of water. Articles made from fibers low in specific gravity are lighter in mass per unit of volume than are those containing a denser fiber.

Specific gravity is important in the processing of fibers and in the designing of fabrics. Low specific gravity is one of the attributes that make it possible to have high bulk and light weight in the textured yarns.

Strength

Tensile strength is the ability of a material to withstand tension. It is expressed in terms of the amount of force required to break a fiber, yarn, or fabric of a given cross-sectional area (pounds per square inch). In the case of fibers or yarns, the strength is usually measured as *tenacity* and is expressed in terms of force per unit of linear density, i.e., grams per denier. In the case of fabrics, strength may be expressed as *breaking*

strength (breaking load) which is the resistance to rupture by tension, i.e., pounds.

Important as the tenacity of fibers is to the completed yarn or fabric, the carry-over contribution of fiber strength to the completed yarn or fabric will also depend on such factors as fiber length, fineness, and yarn twist, in addition to fabric construction. Yarn size and fabric construction being equal, the stronger fiber will produce the stronger fabric. However, low tensile strength of a fiber can be compensated for in construction of yarn and fabric and in finishing processes. Wool is an example of a comparatively weak fiber that can be made into strong and durable fabrics if enough fibers are used to make a comparatively heavy fabric. Higher fiber strength does allow the construction of a greater variety of fabric weights and designs.

Of the natural fibers, silk, linen, and ramie are outstanding in regard to strength. There is a wide range between the high and low values reported for these fibers because there is less uniformity than in manufactured fibers.

Many of the man-made fibers such as rayon, nylon, and polyester, are produced in high-tenacity forms, as well as in regular-tenacity forms. These high-tenacity forms are produced for special purposes (tires, for example). The high-tenacity yarns are characterized by considerably higher strength than that of regular-tenacity yarns.

Wet Strength

Wet strength for fibers is expressed in the same units discussed above under *Strength*.

Cotton, linen, and ramie are outstanding fibers in that they gain in strength when wet. This property makes them relatively easy to launder. Silk and wool decrease in strength when wet.

Among the man-made fibers, the cellulosics and cellulose acetates—rayon, acetate, and triacetate

—all show a considerable decrease in strength when wet. This fact should be considered in the care and handling and particularly in the cleaning of these fabrics. The man-made fibers—nylon, the acrylics, and the polyesters—generally maintain substantially the same strength, whether wet or dry. This property is due to the fibers' low moisture regain and hygroscopicity (that is, the ability of the fibers to absorb and retain moisture).

Moisture Regain

Most textile fibers absorb some moisture from the surrounding atmosphere. The amount absorbed is referred to as the fiber's moisture regain. This property is extremely important in manufacturing, dyeing, and finishing processes.

Moisture regain of a fiber is defined by the American Society for Testing and Materials as "the amount of moisture in a material determined under prescribed conditions and expressed as a percentage of the weight of the moisture-free specimen." [1]

While there appears to be a relationship between the moisture regain of the fiber and the maximum amount of water which a fabric can hold, yarn and fabric construction play much more important parts in this property than does fiber content. For example, a bulky acrylic sweater may be much slower to dry than a medium-weight cotton fabric. In general, however, fibers with low moisture regains will show small or no differences in properties such as strength and elasticity when they become wet.

Moisture absorption is related to ease of dye-ability and to freedom from the buildup of static electricity. It also plays a part in the comfort of clothing made from the various fibers. The high ability of wool to absorb moisture from the body or the atmosphere accounts for much of its comfort. Manufacturing processes such as bulking of yarns, or finishing processes such as anti-static finishes, are applied to fibers of low moisture regain to help them achieve some of the properties of fibers that have natural moisture regain.

[1] Standard Definitions of Terms Relating to Textile Materials, D123-73, American Society for Testing and Materials, *1973 Book of ASTM Standards*, Part 24, p. 31.

Extensibility, Elasticity, and Abrasion Resistance

Extensibility is the property of a material which permits it to be extended or elongated when force is applied. Elasticity is the property by virtue of which a material recovers its original size and shape immediately after removal of the stress causing deformation. Fibers are complex in their extension and elastic properties. A chart on page 4 indicates the range of these values for various fibers.

A fiber's ability to extend, and its ability to return to its original size and shape when the load is removed, are of extreme importance in considering such end-use requirements as abrasion-resistance, wear-resistance, wrinkle-resistance, shape-retention, and resilience.

Nylon is an outstanding fiber because it exhibits high strength as well as high extension. Because it maintains these properties in repeated stressing, nylon has very high abrasion-resistance. Wool's ability to extend under low loads and to return to its original dimension upon load removal are some of the reasons for its excellent wear-resistance. Glass is a good example of a fiber which is outstanding in its high strength but because it is so inextensible there are severe limitations to its use. Fibers with very low elongations (such as glass) usually have very poor resistance to abrasion in the flexed or bent state.

Elasticity helps fabrics to conform to specific contours of the body and to maintain their original shape in use and wear. The elastic recovery of a fiber is dependent upon how much it is stretched, how long it is held in the stretched state, and the length of time it has to recover. Most fibers have very high recovery values when stretched only one or two percent but have less complete recovery when stretched four or five percent. The fit of nylon and silk hose results from inherent elastic recovery of the fibers.

Fibers with low elasticity (cotton and linen, for example) wrinkle easily in their normal state. For many end-uses, therefore, fabrics of these fibers are treated chemically to improve their crease- and wrinkle-resistance. Cotton may also be made into crepe yarns, or woven into fabrics such as seersucker or terry cloth, in which the weave hinders or disguises wrinkling.

CHEMICAL AND PHYSICAL PROPERTIES OF SOME TEXTILE FIBERS[1]

Fiber (*denotes trademark name)	Specific Gravity	Tenacity[2] (grams per denier)	Tenacity (Wet)[2] (grams per denier)	Moisture Regain (percent)	Extensibility[3] (percent)	Elasticity[4] (percent)	Safe[5] Ironing
Cotton	1.54	3-4.9	3.3-6.4	7-8	3-7	74(2) 45(5)	425
Linen	1.5	2.4-7	—	12	3	—	450
Silk	1.25	2.8-5.2	2.5-4.5	11	13-31	92(2) 33(20)	300
Wool	1.32	1-1.7	0.8-1.6	13-17	25-35	99(2) 63(20)	300
Acetate	1.32	1.3-1.5	1.2-1.4	6	23-24	48-65(4)	350
*Arnel triacetate	1.3	0.8-1.2	0.8-1	3.2	26-40	65(5)	400
Acrylic							
*Acrilan	1.17	2-2.7	1.6-2.2	1.5	34-50	99(2) 89(5)	300
*Creslan	1.18	2-3	1.6-2.7	1-1.5	35-45	55-65(3) 40-60(5)	300
*Orlon	1.16	2.2-2.6	1.8-2.1	1.5	20-28	—	300
*Zefran II and *Zefkrome	1.18	2.9-3.6	2.3-2.9	1.5-2.5	35-39	86(3) 58(10)	400 350
Anidex							
*Anim/8, monofilament	1.22	0.4-0.45	—	0.514	400-475	—	
Glass							
single filament	2.55	15.3-19.9	15.3-19.9	None	4.8-5.3	100	
multifilament	2.5	9.6	6.7	None	3.1	100	
Modacrylic							
*Dynel	1.3	3.5-4.2	3.5-4.2	0.4	14-34	100(2) 98(5)	225
*Kynol, staple	1.25	1.7	1.6	5	50	99(1) 95(5)	
*SEF, staple	1.35	1.7-2.6	1.5-2.4	2.5	40-60	100(1) 99(5)	
*Verel	1.33-1.37	2-2.8	2-2.7	3-4.25	25-43	88(4) 55(10)	275
Nylon 6							
regular monofilament	1.14	4-7	3.7-6.2	2.8-5	17-45	99-100(2-100)	300
staple	1.14	3.8-5.5	—	2.8-5	37-50	100(2)	300

Fiber							
Nylon 66							
regular monofilament	1.14	3-6	2.6-5.2	4.2-4.5	25-65	100(5) 99-100(10)	350
staple and tow	1.14	3.5-7.2	3-6.1	4.2-4.5	16-66	—	
*Nomex	1.38	4-5.3	3-4.1	6.5	22-32	—	
*Qiana	1.03	2.7-3	—	2.5	26-36	—	
Olefin							
Polyethylene, monofilament		3.5-7	3.5-7	0.01	20-80	95(5) 88(10)	
Polypropylene-isotactic							
monofilament	0.9-0.91	3.5-7	3.5-7	0.01-0.1	14-30	98(5) 95(10)	150
staple and tow	0.9-0.91	3-6.5	3-6.5	0.01-0.1	20-80	97-100(2) 94-100(5)	
Polyesters, regular tenacity							
*Anavor, filament	1.38	4.5	4.5	0.4	30-32	—	
*Avlin, staple	1.38	3.5-5	3.5-5	0.4	35-50	90-95(2) 55-65(5)	
*Dacron, staple	1.38	2.2-6	2.2-6	0.4-0.8	12-55	100(1)	325
*Encron, filament	1.38	4.4-5	4.4-5	0.4	27-36	55-65(5)	
*Fortrel, staple	1.38	4.8	4.8	0.4	45-55	75-80(5)	325
*Kodel, staple	1.38	4.5-5.5	4.5-5.5	0.4	35-45	75-85(2) 35-45(5)	325
*Quintess, staple	1.38	4.5-5.5	4.5-5.5	0.4	40-50	—	
*Spectran, staple	1.38	3.3-6.1	—	0.4	30-55	92(2) 75(5)	
*Trevira, staple	1.38	3.1-6.6	3.1-6.6	0.4	18-55	67-86(2) 57-74(5)	300
*Vycron, staple	1.38	3.8-5.8	3.8-5.8	0.6	22-67	44(5) 33(10)	
Rayon							
Viscose, regular tenacity	1.5-1.53	0.73-2.6	0.7-1.8	13	15-30	30-74(4)	375
Viscose, medium tenacity	1.5-1.53	2.4-3.2	1.2-1.9	13	15-20	97(2)	375
Viscose, high tenacity	1.5-1.53	3-5.7	1.9-4.3	13	9-26	70-100(2)	375
Cuprammonium	1.52-1.54	1.7-2.3	0.95-1.35	12.5	7-23	17-75	375
*Avril	1.5	5.1	3.5	13	18	—	
*Nupron	1.53	5.1	3.5	13	14	65(2)	
*Xena	1.5-1.53	5.1	3.3	11-12	18	—	
*Zantrel 700	1.51	5	3	11.5-12.5	15	95(2)	

NOTE: See footnotes at end of chart, page 6.

Fiber							
Saran	1.7	up to 1.5		None	15-25	—	150
Spandex							
*Glospan, multifilament	1.2	0.7	0.6-0.9	<1	600-700	99(50) 98(200)	
*Lycra, monofilament	1.21	0.7-0.9	—	1.3	444-555	97(50)	300
*Numa, multifilament	1.2	0.6-0.9	—	1	500-600	98(300)	
*Unel, fused multifilament	1.2	0.55-0.85	—	1.3	500-700	96-98.5(50)	
Flurocarbon							
*Teflon, staple	2.1	1.2-1.4	1.2-1.4	—	15-33	—	
*Teflon, monofilament	2.1	0.5	0.5	—	52	—	
Biconstituent Fiber							
*Source (biconstituent of nylon/polyester polymer)	1.22	up to 9	4	2.7	45 maximum	100(4)	

[1] Because natural fibers inevitably vary in properties and man-made fibers may be produced in various forms, values given should be interpreted as indicating order of magnitude of the fibers as used in textile applications.
[2] Tested at 21°C (70°F) with relative humidity 65 percent.
[3] Percentage of elongation at 65 percent relative humidity.
[4] Percentage of recovery from strain indicated.
[5] Degree Fahrenheit recommended by the Burlington Industries Research Center on the basis of its own research tests.

SOURCES:

Textile Chemistry and Testing in the Laboratory, Rose Padgett, Southern Illinois University at Carbondale, University Bookstore, 1973. (Cotton, silk, wool. . . specific gravity and elastic recovery)

Fiber Facts 1969-70. Philadelphia: FMC Corporation, American Viscose Division, 1969. (Conditioned and wet tenacities, moisture regain, and elongation)

"1972 Man-Made Fiber Chart," Noreen Heimbold, *Textile World,* 120: 69-92 (August 1972) (Data on man-made fibers)

Textile Fibers

Today, consumers find themselves increasingly in need of information on which to base their selections of textile products. Familiarity with the general characteristics of broad groups of fibers from which fabrics and other textile products are made can aid consumers, teachers, students, and researchers in knowing what to expect of these fibers, alone or in combination with others.

Fabrics, carpeting, or other textile products, when made of one particular fiber, generally retain the properties of the fiber with possibly some modification due to the structure of the yarn, structure of the fabric, or the finish. When two or more fibers are combined, some individual properties may be lost or modified.

This chapter lists the major properties of fibers as *advantages* or *limitations*. The fibers are classified as *natural fibers* and *man-made fibers*. The natural fibers are grouped in two broad classes: cellulosic fibers (cotton, flax, hemp, jute, ramie) and protein fibers (silk, wool, speciality hair). The man-made fibers are grouped in the 19 generic classifications defined by the Federal Trade Commission in the Rules and Regulations for the Textile Fibers Products Identification Act (1958) as amended to 1969. (See **Textile Legislation and Trade Rules and Regulations,** pages 101 to 105.)

Natural Fibers (Cellulosic)

Cotton

Cotton fibers grow in the boll or seed pod of cotton plants which are cultivated in warm climates. Different species of cotton plants produce fibers of different lengths.

Long fibers are used in better quality fabrics because they can be spun into fine, smooth, lustrous, and comparatively strong yarns. Short fibers produce coarser yarns which can be made into fabrics that are durable but less fine and lustrous. Fiber lengths are designated as:

Extra long staple [1] . . . . 1⅜ to 2 inches
(3.49 to 5.08 cm)
Long staple . . . . 1⅛ to 1⅜ inches
(2.86 to 3.49 cm)
Medium staple . . . . 1 to 1⅛ inches
(2.54 to 2.86 cm)
Short staple . . . . ⅞ to 1 inch
(2.22 to 2.54 cm)

There are two general categories for American cotton: *American-Upland* and *American-Egyptian*. Upland varieties include Coker, Deltapine, Acala, and Stoneville. The best known American-Egyptian variety is Pima.

Advantages of cotton: (1) Fabrics made from cotton offer a wide selection of weights, textures, colors, and patterns. For example, among the sheer cottons are chiffon, organdy, lawn, batiste, voile. Medium weight includes poplin, denim, sailcloth, flannel, terry cloth. The heavyweight cottons include tweed, knit fabrics, brocade, corduroy, velveteen.

(2) Textured effects may be achieved either by yarn, fabric structure, or by special finishing treatments. Cotton may be mercerized and polished to improve luster and crispness.

(3) Cotton fabrics may be dyed and printed easily and evenly.

(4) Cotton also has a special affinity for vat and reactive dyes and is available in a wide

---

[1] Staple, as a textile term, refers to fiber length. Fibers, natural or man-made, that are so short they are customarily measured in inches or centimeters rather than yards or meters are called staple. Filament is the term for fibers that can be measured in yards or meters as, for example, silk and man-made fibers. Some man-made fibers are manufactured in staple and filament lengths.

Advantages of cotton (Continued)

selection of brilliant and subdued colors and prints.

(5) Cotton is comfortable to wear primarily because of high absorbency and wickability (ability to transmit perspiration moisture away from body). Freedom from static electricity lends comfort.

(6) Durability and wear life are excellent with no pilling or melting, and little, if any, seam slippage.

(7) Fabrics can be laundered or drycleaned. Cotton is one of the few fibers that increases in strength when wet. White and colorfast fabrics may be washed in hot water (120°-212°F) and dried at high temperatures (160°-200°F). They are resistant to strong alkalies and respond readily to chlorine or other types of bleaches but may be weakened by excessive use of chlorine bleaches.

(8) Cotton fabrics can be stabilized mechanically and chemically.

(9) Fabrics are receptive to many chemical and additive-type finishes. Cotton is the component, when blended with man-made fibers, that reacts chemically with durable press finishes to give wash-and-wear properties and resistance to wrinkling. Other chemical treatments include resistance to perspiration odors, mildew, rot, weather, fire, and water. Chemical finishing involves the chemical reaction of the finish with cotton cellulose, whereas in additive finishing the finish impregnates or coats the fibers. Chemical finishes are durable. Additive finishes may be durable or nondurable depending upon the end-use of the fabric and the finish employed.

Limitations of cotton: (1) Untreated cotton fabrics lack elasticity and resilience. They crease and wrinkle easily. Treatment with a chemical finish can provide wrinkle-resistance at the expense of some degree of tear strength and abrasion resistance.

(2) Untreated cottons are degraded by microorganisms (mildew and rot), sunlight, and strong acids.

(3) Untreated cotton fabrics are flammable.

Flax

Flax fibers surround the woody core of the flax plant, a tall thin stalk, grown in cool, damp climates. Retting, a soaking process in chemically treated water, dislodges the fibers by destroying the pectic gum holding the fibers. After the flax has dried, scutching separates the fibers and the woody portions. Hackling is the combing of the long fibers, called line, and the carding of the short fibers called tow. Both retting and scutching are unique processes for the bast fibers. Line fibers may average 18 to 20 inches (45.72 to 50.8 cm) in length. Fine grades of linen fabric are made from these long fibers. Tow fibers are used in novelty, homespun, and textured yarns.

Advantages of flax: (1) Fiber is extremely strong.

(2) Fabric gains in strength when wet, and this added strength contributes to easy laundering.

(3) Linen fabrics can be cool and comfortable to wear because of high moisture absorption and wickability.

(4) Linens are smooth and therefore do not lint.

(5) Fabrics made from flax are moth-resistant and resistant to alkaline substances and reagents.

(6) Linens can be laundered or drycleaned, depending on dye, finish, design application, and garment construction.

(7) White linen may be bleached with chlorine-type bleaches unless finish is chlorine-retentive. Overbleaching weakens fiber.

(8) Unless resin-treated, linens withstand high ironing temperatures.

Limitations of flax: (1) Untreated linen fabrics lack resiliency and elasticity. Chemical finishes can be applied to impart crease or wrinkle-resistance, but at the expense of lowering tear strength and abrasion-resistance.

(2) Fibers are stiff with poor resistance to flex abrasion; consequently garments often show wear at edges and seams where fabric is bent.

(3) Pressed crease retention is poor.

(4) Untreated linen fabrics are flammable.

Hemp

Hemp is grown in the United States, Russia, Yugoslavia, and Poland. In its color and luster it is similar to flax. Because it is quite resistant to salt water, it is used primarily for cordage. It is also used for fishing lines, nets, sailcloths, and other items that must withstand weather.

Advantages of hemp: (1) Fiber is strong.
(2) It is resistant to salt water.

Limitations of hemp: (1) Fiber is harsh and stiff.
(2) Hemp is comparatively expensive.
(3) It is damaged by bleaching.

Jute

Jute is a bast fiber from the stalk of a plant which is grown primarily in India. The fiber is separated in a process similar to that used on flax. The fibers are cut into the lengths desired by the manufacturer.

Jute is a coarse fiber used in the construction of carpet backing, burlap bagging, and other burlap fabric.

Advantages of jute: (1) It can be processed with finishing agents to increase its durability and resistance to rot, microbial decomposition, water, and fire.
(2) Jute can be treated with caustic soda to give it wool-like characteristics.

Limitations of jute: (1) Jute fibers are the weakest of the important textile fibers.
(2) Jute is naturally very harsh and difficult to bleach.
(3) It is susceptible to microbial decomposition.
(4) Unless especially treated, jute cannot be drycleaned or washed; hence use is limited.

Ramie

Ramie (also known as China grass) comes from the stalk of a semitropical plant. Chemical and mechanical methods separate the fibers from the woody stalk. Ramie fibers range from about 2 to 18 inches long (5.08-45.72 cm); the longer fibers are processed in the same way as flax. Shorter fibers may be processed on cotton, wool, or other machinery for staple fibers.

Advantages of ramie: (1) This fiber can be made into strong, lustrous fabrics of various weights because of the fiber's natural strength and luster.
(2) Fabrics made of ramie dye fairly easily.
(3) They are resistant to alkalies and mildew.
(4) Fabrics can be laundered, wetcleaned, drycleaned, depending on dyes, finish, and design application.

Advantages of ramie (Continued)
(5) White ramie may be bleached with chlorine-type bleaches (but should not be overbleached).
(6) Ramie withstands high ironing temperatures.

Limitations of ramie: (1) The supply and availability are limited.
(2) Fibers are damaged easily by strong acid substances and reagents.
(3) Ramie is low in elasticity and resilience; hence wrinkles very easily.
(4) Fibers are stiff and brittle, have poor flex abrasion-resistance, and tend to crack along folds.
(5) Ramie fabrics are more expensive than cotton and linen.

Natural Fibers (Protein)

Silk

Silk is the fiber excreted by the silkworm (the larval stage of the moth *Bombyx mori*) when it builds its cocoon. Cultivated silkworms are fed on mulberry leaves and then stifled by heat so that they will not emerge and break their cocoons. The cocoons are soaked in warm water to soften the gum that binds the cocoon together. Then the silk fiber is carefully unwound (reeled) in a continuous filament 400 to 1300 yards (365.76 to 1188.72 meters) in length.

Several cocoons are unwound at one time, and the filaments are twisted together to produce a yarn. A subsequent treatment may be used to remove the gum either partially or completely.

Douppioni. Occasionally two cocoons accidentally grow together, and sometimes cocoons are deliberately placed so they will grow together. The resulting fiber filaments are joined at intervals, thus producing a thick-and-thin yarn. This property is used to advantage in making certain textured silk fabrics. Silk shantung is a typical example.

Silk Noil are short fibers from broken or defective cocoons. They are spun by a method similar to that used for cotton. These short silk fibers may be called silk noil or silk waste. They may be blended with other natural fibers or with man-made fibers to produce color contrast or to introduce an interesting texture. They are frequently used in thick-and-thin yarns.

Tussah or Wild Silk. Uncultivated silkworms may feed on oak leaves or cherry leaves instead of mulberry. The resulting fibers tend to be tan in color and cannot be bleached. These fibers are also more coarse and uneven than cultivated silk. They are called tussah or wild silk. The fabrics produced are textured and uneven. The fibers may be dyed dark colors but not light tints.

Advantages of silk: (1) Fabrics are luxurious in appearance and feel.

(2) Silks can be dyed and printed readily for beautiful, brilliant shades.

(3) Silks are adaptable to a variety of constructions, from very sheer drapeable fabrics to heavy, stiff, bouffant fabrics.

(4) Fibers are very strong in relation to their filament fineness.

(5) Fabrics are moderately resilient and also elastic; therefore, moderately wrinkle-resistant.

(6) Silks are very absorbent; hence comfortable to wear.

(7) Garments made of silk can be laundered, wetcleaned, or drycleaned depending on dye, finish, design, and garment construction.

(8) White silk fabrics may be bleached with hydrogen peroxide or sodium perborate bleaches.

Limitations of silk: (1) Sunlight and perspiration weaken fabrics.

(2) Many dyes used on silk are affected by sunlight and perspiration; some dyes bleed during laundering.

(3) Silks may be damaged by certain acid and alkaline substances and reagents.

(4) Silks generate static electricity that makes fabrics cling.

(5) Some fabrics water-spot readily.

(6) Silks can be attacked by insects, especially carpet beetles.

(7) Strong soaps and high ironing temperatures tend to weaken and yellow fabrics.

(8) Silks may also yellow with age or exposure to sunlight or bleaching in a chlorine bleach.

Weighted Silk

This silk fabric has a metallic weighting, usually tin salts loading or an adulterating material in the fabric.

Advantages of weighted silk: (1) In some cases, weighted silk may have more drapeability

Advantages of weighted silk (Continued)

than a pure-dye (unweighted silk) of comparable construction.

(2) Fabrics are less expensive in most cases when compared to pure-dye silk fabrics of comparable constructions.

(3) Weighted silk can be laundered, wetcleaned, or drycleaned depending on dye, amount and kind of weighting, design application, and garment construction.

Limitations of weighted silk: (1) It is not so serviceable as pure-dye silk. The greater the degree of weighting, the less the degree of serviceability.

(2) Weighted silk may crack and split with very little use or wear or drycleaning.

(3) Perspiration and sunlight quickly weaken weighted silks.

(4) Spots and stains are more difficult to remove from weighted silks than from pure-dye silks. Reagents used for removal may react with weighting material and cause fabric damage.

Wool

Wool is the fiber from the fleece of the sheep or lamb. Hair of certain goats or camels may be classified as wool under the Wool Products Labeling Act (1939). The better quality wool is clipped annually from live sheep. A poorer quality (pulled wool) is removed from the hide of slaughtered sheep. The wool is sorted, graded, and then washed or cleaned to remove dirt and natural oils.

Yarns made of wool may be classified as woolen or worsted, depending upon the manufacturing process used. Short fibers, which may be two inches (5.08 cm) or less in length, are made into soft, fuzzy woolen yarns. Long wool fibers, which may be two to eight inches (5.08 to 20.32 cm) long, are used for worsted yarns, which are smoother and firmer than woolen yarns.

Advantages of wool: (1) Wool is warm and comfortable. Its resiliency and natural absorbency impart a dry warmth; wool never feels clammy.

(2) Wool is also cool in lightweight fabrics. It breathes and thereby lets heat out and air in to keep the body dry and cool.

(3) Wool absorbs moisture readily without making the wearer feel cold.

Advantages of wool (Continued)

(4) Wood fibers are very resilient and elastic; hence fabrics naturally resist wrinkling.

(5) Wool dyes easily, permitting a wide range of colors with no "frosting" or change of color.

(6) Fibers are fairly resistant to acid substances.

(7) Woolens are supple and yield with body movements. Fabrics tailor well because of ability to be molded to shape. Crease and stitch marks easily steam out.

(8) Fibers are naturally water-repellent and flame-resistant.

(9) Wool may be laundered, wetcleaned, or drycleaned depending on the dyes, finish, garment design, and findings.

Limitations of wool: (1) It is very sensitive to alkaline substances.

(2) Fabrics are readily attacked by moths and carpet beetles unless treated to resist them.

(3) Wool requires some special handling in laundering and drycleaning to prevent felting and relaxation shrinkage. Special finishes reduce felting and shrinkage hazards.

(4) Chlorine bleaches may yellow or even dissolve wool.

(5) Wool must be pressed with steam to preserve appearance of the fabric.

(6) Woolen garments tend to stretch during wear and excessive handling while wet. (Garments should be allowed to "rest" about 24 hours between wearings to allow garments to return to shape.)

Specialty Hair Fibers

Specialty hair fibers are obtained from several families or species of animals. They are used with wool or other fibers to produce special effects or to give additional beauty, color, softness, or luster. Some may be used alone.

The Camel Family. Several different fabrics belong to this group.

Alpaca. Gray and fawn-colored fabrics predominate, but fabrics are also available in white, black, or coffee color.

Camel's hair. Genuine camel's hair fabrics are very expensive. They should not be confused with the wool fabrics that are made to resemble genuine camel's hair.

The Camel Family (Continued)

Guanaco. Sometimes called fibers of the wild. Fabrics using this fiber are soft, luxurious, and expensive.

Llama. True brown fabrics predominate. A few are light beige.

Vicuña. Coats made of vicuña sell in the same price range as fur coats. A very limited amount of vicuña is available, because the animal cannot be domesticated and the Peruvian government has made attempts to prevent the extinction of the vicuña.

Fur-bearing Animals. Fabrics are being sold currently that combine beaver, mink, seal, or Angora (rabbit) in a variety of items.

The Goat Family. Two well known fabrics are made from fibers obtained from the goat family.

Angora goat. Better known as **mohair.** This should not be confused with Angora rabbit hair. Mohair is used in fabrics ranging from heavy drapery and upholstery fabrics to very sheer dress fabrics.

Cashmere goat. A natural fiber obtained from the fine underdown of the Kashmir goat found in the high plateaus of inner Asia. A small amount of the fiber comes from Kashmir, India. China and Outer Mongolia produce the greatest amount of the fiber. The natural color of cashmere is white, gray, or tan. It can be dyed from very light pastel colors to dark colors, blue, brown, and black.

The word "Kashmir" generally refers to a lower grade of cashmere. Over the years, however, the words "Kashmir" and "cashmere" have been used interchangeably.

The annual clip of the Kashmir goat is very small in relation to the demand. The inaccessibility of the areas where cashmere is produced and the primitive methods of transportation contribute to its cost.

There are some limitations to cashmere:

(1) The fabric is susceptible to abrasion in wear. In garments, effects of wear usually occur first at neckline, cuffs, front opening, and edge of pockets. The seat may show abrasion, too.

(2) Small dark hairs often appear throughout pastel-colored cashmere fabrics. These are the

Specialty Hair Fibers (Continued)
guard hairs that were not removed from the fine down fibers before they were spun into yarn.

(3) Cashmere is subject to pilling (a term used to describe the bunching together of surface fibers into a ball). This is usually more noticeable in knit goods than in woven cashmere and occurs most frequently in the underarm area where the sleeve rubs against the body.

Musk Ox. Qiviut, the underwool fiber of the domesticated ox of Alaska, is used in hand-knitted products which are soft and lacy in design. The products are expensive due to the limited amounts of qiviut that the musk ox produces annually.

Reindeer. The hair fibers are used to give textured effects.

Man-Made Fibers [1]

The American Society for Testing and Materials defines the term *man-made fibers* as "a class name for various genera of fibers (including filaments) produced from fiber-forming substances which may be (1) polymers synthesized by man from simple chemical compounds, (2) modified or transformed natural polymers, and (3) glasses." [2]

The generic names of these man-made fibers are as follows: acetate, acrylic, anidex, aramid, azlon,* glass, lastrile,* metallic, modacrylic, novoloid, nylon, nytril,* olefin, polyester, rayon, rubber, saran, spandex, triacetate, vinal,* and vinyon. (The names marked with an * signify fibers not produced in the United States.)

Most man-made fibers are thermoplastic, which means that they are softened by heat—a characteristic that must be taken into account in the manipulation of the fiber in production processes, in clothing construction, and care.

---

[1] Generic names and italicized definitions in this section are those established by the Federal Trade Commission under Rule 7, Rules and Regulations under the Textile Fiber Products Identification Act.

[2] Standard Definitions of Terms Relating to Textile Materials (D123-73), *1973 Book of ASTM Standards*, Part 24 or Part 25.

Each group of fibers also has certain advantages and limitations. Fibers of the same generic name but produced by different companies may have like properties but in varying degrees. There are, however, sufficient traits in common to make a knowledge of them helpful to the consumer in the interest of wise selection and satisfactory use. Just as in the past the consumer became familiar with the characteristics of the natural fibers, he may now profitably gain by understanding the characteristics and advantages and limitations of man-made fibers.

The consumer should keep in mind that a fiber property which may seem to be a limitation is not necessarily a disadvantage if the fiber is used in a suitable end product.

The generic types of man-made fibers as defined by the Federal Trade Commission do not break down easily into logical groups; however these rather arbitrary classifications may prove helpful:

Cellulosic fibers: acetate, rayon, triacetate

Non-cellulosic fibers: acrylic, anidex, aramid, lastrile, modacrylic, novoloid, nylon, nytril, olefin, polyester, rubber,** saran, spandex, vinal, vinyon.

Fibers manufactured from non-fibrous natural substances: azlon, glass, metallic fibers, rubber** (rubber fibers indicated with ** are included in two classifications since the fiber-forming substance may be made of natural or synthetic rubber).

The Textile Fiber Products Identification Act, which became effective in March, 1960, requires identification of fiber content and percentage of each fiber in textile merchandise. Consumers are thus informed of the *fiber* or *fibers* contained in textile articles. Labels must also give generic names of fibers, but trademark names are optional.

Although no publication can keep completely up to date about fibers and their adaptations and uses, an understanding of the current situation helps in the evaluation of future developments.

Acetate

Acetate is a manufactured fiber in which the fiber-forming substance is cellulose acetate. Where not less than 92 percent of the hydroxyl groups are acetylated, the term triacetate may be used as a generic description of the fiber.

Cellulose Acetate. Purified wood pulp is usually the starting material for cellulose acetate. This starting material, cellulose, is treated with acetic acid and acetic anhydride. The resulting solution is poured into water and coagulated into flakes. The flakes are dried and dissolved in acetone, forming a colorless syrupy solution. This solution is extruded downward into a warm air chamber, and as the acetone evaporates, the pull of gravity causes the filaments to stretch slightly. The filaments may be chopped into short staple fibers for use in spun yarns.

Special cross-section fibers provide greater reflective surface when woven into a fabric. These filaments are flat and can reflect light to a greater degree than can a round filament.

Cellulose Triacetate. Cellulose triacetate is produced from purified cotton linters or wood pulp activated with acetic and sulfuric acids. The product is treated with acetic anhydride in the presence of acetic acid and precipitated into water. The triacetate flakes are dissolved in methylene chloride and extruded with minimum stretching. Heat treatment is essential to make triacetate yarns more dimensionally stable. This heat treatment may be done after the yarn is woven into fabric.

One of the most noticeable differences between cellulose triacetate and regular cellulose acetate fibers is the higher temperature at which triacetate can be ironed.

Advantages common to generic group of acetate fibers: (1) Can be given durable surface effects by hot calendering.

(2) Have luxurious soft feel.

(3) Have silky appearance.

(4) Have excellent draping qualities.

(5) Can be solution-dyed and thereby increase color fastness to light, atmospheric gas-fading, crocking, perspiration, and cleaning.

(6) Resist mildew and moths.

(7) May be bleached with hydrogen peroxide or sodium perborate bleaches at temperatures not above 90°F.

(8) May be laundered, wetcleaned, or drycleaned depending on dyes, finishes, decorative design, and garment design.

(9) Provide many interesting cross-dye effects in fiber-blended fabrics because the dye char-

acteristics of acetate are different from those of other fibers.

Limitations common to generic group of acetate fibers: (1) Are heat sensitive.

(2) Some dyes are subject to atmospheric fading.

(3) Have poor abrasion resistance.

(4) Generate static electricity.

(5) Have low conditioned strength.

(6) Lose some strength when wet.

(7) Are soluble in acetone and acetic acid.

(8) Are weakened by lengthy exposure to light —dull fibers especially.

(9) Require special class of dyes.

(10) Absorb little moisture.

(11) Are moderately flammable.

Advantages of special cross-section acetate fibers: (1) Provide shimmering effects.

(2) Combine well with regular acetate, silk, wool, nylon.

(3) Can be drycleaned.

Limitations of special cross-section acetate fibers: (1) Have lower strength and stretch than regular acetate.

(2) Fabrics are more fragile than regular acetate of same construction.

(3) Present some dye problems.

Advantages of triacetate fibers: (1) Can be heat-set.

(2) Take dye readily.

(3) Have good wrinkle resistance.

(4) Resist glazing during ironing.

(5) Can be given durable crease- and pleat-retention.

(6) Anti-static finish can be built into fiber.

(7) Can be ironed at moderate ironing temperatures.

(8) May be bleached with peroxygen-type bleaches.

(9) Are machine washable.

(10) Dry with excellent stability.

Limitations of triacetate fibers: (1) Are susceptible to gas-fading unless heat-treated.

(2) Have low conditioned and wet strength.

(3) Have poor abrasion resistance.

(4) Are damaged by light.

(5) Are soluble in acetone and acetic acid.

(6) Are moderately flammable.

SOME ACETATE FIBERS AND YARNS

Trademark Name	Description	Manufacturer*
Arnel	Triacetate staple and filament yarn	Celanese
Celanese acetate	Bright and dull filament yarn; staple; voluminous yarn; thick-and-thin filament; textured filament; crystal	Celanese
Celaperm	Solution-dyed yarn	Celanese
Arnel-plus-nylon	Blended filament yarn	du Pont
Acele	Filament yarn, natural and color-sealed	du Pont
Color-sealed acetate	Solution-dyed fiber	du Pont
Estron	Filament yarn	Eastman
Chromspun	Solution-dyed fiber	Eastman
Avisco acetate	Acetate filament yarn and staple	FMC

*See Appendix for full name and address.

Acrylic

Acrylic—a manufactured fiber in which the fiber-forming substance is any long chain synthetic polymer composed of at least 85 percent by weight of acrylonitrile units ($-CH_2-CH-$).
$$\underset{CN}{|}$$

Acrylic fibers are made from a special group of vinyl compounds, primarily acrylonitrile.

The acrylonitrile is copolymerized with from 5 to 15 percent of a second monomer. This second monomer may differ in chemical type from one fiber producer to another or even between two types of acrylic fibers produced by the same manufacturer. The use of different types of monomers to copolymerize with the acrylonitrile can produce fibers with different softening points and attractions for different types of dyes.

The polymer is dissolved in a solvent, usually dimethyl formamide, and extruded through spinnerets. *Orlon* (du Pont) is dryspun; that is, the fiber is extruded into a warm chamber where the solvent evaporates. Other acrylics such as *Acrilan*, *Creslan*, and *Zefran* are wetspun— the spinning solution is extruded into a bath which removes the solvent and solidifies the fibers. After spinning, the fiber is drawn slightly to improve

strength and dimensional stability. Heat setting, in either yarn or fabric form, is necessary to achieve good stability.

A bicomponent *Orlon* fiber is also produced. In bicomponent fibers, two acrylic polymers which differ slightly in heat sensitivity and water absorption are joined to form a single fiber. Thus, one side of the fiber will shrink more upon heating than will the other. This forms a final fiber with a three-dimensional spiral crimp. Garments made from *Orlon* bicomponent acrylic should be either dried flat, or preferably tumble-dried at moderate heat to restore the fiber crimp and to keep the garment from stretching.

Acrylic fibers are thermoplastic (that is, they can be made plastic by the application of heat), they have low moisture regain, are low in density, and can be made into bulky fabrics. They wash and dry easily and are dimensionally stable.

Some representative acrylic fibers and yarns are *Creslan* (staple and tow, American Cyanamid), *Acrilan* (staple and tow, Monsanto), *Zefkrome* and *Zefran* (staple and tow, Dow Badische), and *Orlon* (staple and tow, du Pont).

Trademark names of *Orlon* bicomponent acrylic fibers are *Wintuk* and *Sayelle*.

Advantages of acrylic fibers: (1) Have low density.

(2) Can be heat-set.

(3) Have good bulking properties.

(4) Are resilient.

(5) Have good pleat-retention and wrinkle-resistance.

(6) Are comparatively dimensionally stable.

(7) Wash easily.

(8) Are resistant to bleaches, dilute acids, alkalies, to weathering and microbiological attack.

(9) Have good dye fastness.

(10) Are thermoplastic.

(11) May be laundered, wetcleaned, or drycleaned, depending on dye, finish, design application, and garment construction.

(12) May be bleached with chlorine-type bleach.

(13) Have moderate abrasion resistance.

Limitations of acrylic fibers: (1) Have low moisture regain or absorption.

(2) Are heat sensitive.

(3) Accumulate static electricity.

(4) May pill in some yarn constructions.

(5) Are moderately flammable.

(6) Have moderate retention of oil-borne stains.

Anidex

Anidex is a manufactured fiber in which the fiber-forming substance is any long chain synthetic polymer composed of at least 50 percent by weight of one or more esters of a monohydric alcohol and acrylic acid, $CH_2{=}CH{-}COOH$.

Anidex is a new generic group of fibers, defined by the Federal Trade Commission in a 1969 amendment to the Textile Fiber Products Identification Act and authorized as of October 31, 1969. Anidex fibers are elastomeric fibers with a chemical base different from that of spandex or rubber.

The first of this generic class to be put out under a brand name is *Anim/8*, developed by Rohm and Haas Company. The properties given below are based on the manufacturer's claims.

Advantages of anidex fibers: (1) They have excellent elastic recovery with warp, fill, and bias stretch that permits freedom in the garment design.

(2) The resiliency of the fibers is not impaired by repeated washings and drycleanings.

(3) White, colored, and printed fabrics containing anidex fibers may be safely chlorine-bleached.

(4) Anidex, when blended with other fibers such as cotton or wool, imparts additional stretch and recovery without changing the appearance or characteristics of the original fiber.

(5) In fiber-blended fabrics, anidex provides good shape retention.

Limitations of anidex fibers: Since the fiber is new and not yet consumer tested in household and apparel uses, the limitations, if any as compared to other fibers, are not known.

Aramid

Aramid is a manufactured fiber in which the fiber-forming substance is a long chain synthetic polyamide in which at least 85 percent of the amide ($-C-NH-$) *linkages are attached directly to two aromatic rings.*

$$\underset{O}{\overset{\|}{C}}$$

Aramid is a new generic group, defined by the Federal Trade Commission in a ruling that became effective as of January 11, 1974. Aramid fibers are polyamides with a chemical base different from that of regular nylon.

The first two fibers to be classed as aramids are *Kevlar (Fiber B)* and *Nomex*, both by du Pont. The properties given below are based on the manufacturer's claims.

Advantages of aramid fibers: (1) *Kevlar* has high strength and a greater stretch resistance than conventional fibers.

(2) *Kevlar* is used in tires and other rubber goods and as reinforcing material for plastic composites.

(3) *Nomex* fiber has resistance to high temperatures and is used in protective clothing.

(4) In paper form, *Nomex* is used as insulation in motors, transformers, and in mechanical aerospace structures.

(5) *Nomex* fiber is used in carpets for aircraft and navy ships.

Limitations of aramid fibers: Since the fibers are new and are still being tested in commercial, industrial, and military uses, the limitations, if any, as compared to other fibers, are not known.

Azlon

Azlon is a manufactured fiber in which the fiber-forming substance is composed of any regenerated naturally occurring proteins.

Azlon fibers are not currently in production in the United States. *Aralac* (casein from milk) and *Vicara* (zein from corn) are examples of azlon that were produced in the United States. Some azlon fibers produced elsewhere are *Fibrolane* (England) and *Merinova* (Italy).

Advantages of azlon fibers: (1) These fibers dye readily and resist moths and mildew.

(2) In blended fabrics azlon fibers contribute wrinkle-resistance, softness, and absorbency, and reduce pilling.

(3) Azlon fibers are dimensionally stable.

(4) They can be bleached with hydrogen peroxide.

Limitations of azlon fibers: (1) They have low strength—wet or dry.

(2) They are affected by alkalies.

Glass Fibers

Glass as a textile is defined by the Federal Trade Commission as a *manufactured fiber in which the fiber-forming substance is glass.*

Glass fibers are produced from a special glass. Silica sand, limestone, soda ash, borax, and other ingredients are melted together. The resulting glass is formed into marbles, inspected for quality, then melted. The glass flows downward through a spinneret at high speed. The continuous filaments are stretched as they cool and are wound on a reel at high speed. When short glass staple fibers are desired, the fibers are broken by a steam jet as they leave the spinneret. These fibers are caught on a revolving drum and then spun into yarn.

Some glass fibers are listed below with trademark names given in italics. For full names and addresses of manufacturers, see Appendix.

Fiberfrax Ceramic Fiber, used in applications requiring high temperature insulation (Carborundum); *Unifab, Uniformat,* and *Unirove* (Ferro); *Beta* and *Fiberglas* (Owens-Corning); *PPG* (PPG Industries, Inc.).

Advantages of glass fibers: (1) They are incombustible.

(2) They are very strong.

(3) Glass fibers are weather- and sun-resistant.

(4) They are not damaged by moths, mildew, or many chemical substances.

(5) Fabrics do not absorb moisture—an important quality in curtain and drapery fabrics.

(6) Glass fabrics shed dust and soil; soil is easily removed unless it is allowed to become ground into the surface of the fabric.

(7) Glass curtains and draperies may be hand-laundered or wetcleaned; they should be finished with steam.

(8) White glass fibers may be bleached with chlorine-type bleaches.

Limitations of glass fibers: (1) Because glass fiber fabrics have low moisture-absorption, dyeing and printing of them are limited. However, recent developments in dyeing glass fibers make it possible to obtain multicolored effects through cross-dyeing fabrics woven from glass fibers with different surface characteristics.

(2) Unless given special treatment, fibers have very low abrasion-resistance. For example, curtains blowing in and out of a window or rubbing against a sill can cause abrasion of fibers. A glass fiber *Beta* (Owens-Corning) is claimed to be more abrasion-resistant because it is spun in a much finer filament size.

(3) In some constructions, seam and yarn slippage may occur because of the smoothness of the yarns.

(4) Fibers are attacked by weak alkaline solutions and by hydrofluoric acid.

(5) Glass fibers are easily damaged by mechanical action in use and in cleaning.

Metallic Fibers

A metallic fiber is *a manufactured fiber composed of metal, plastic-coated metal, metal-coated plastic, or a core completely covered by metal.* Metallic fibers are usually aluminum filaments covered with plastic materials such as cellulose-acetate-butyrate or polyester film. These fibers possess a bright glitter and are available in gold, silver, and a wide range of colors.

Metallic fibers are used in making decorative yarns for apparel fabrics and in home furnishings and domestic fabrics.

Metallic fibers with an electrically conductive metal (aluminum) core laminated to a plastic film have been developed to control static build-up in commercial carpets. The anti-static fibers are incorporated into the yarn during the plying process.

Trademark names of metallic fibers are *Lurex* (Dow Badische) and *Zefstat* anti-static (Dow Badische).

Advantages of metallic fibers: (1) They provide a wide choice of highly decorative yarns.

(2) Fibers coated with a plastic covering are non-tarnishable and can be laundered or dry-cleaned.

Limitations of metallic fibers: They must be ironed at low temperatures because of their plastic coverings. However a polyester film such as *Mylar* (du Pont) will withstand heat better than will an acetate film.

Modacrylic Fibers

Modacrylic is a manufactured fiber in which the fiber-forming substance is any long chain synthetic polymer composed of less than 85 percent but at least 35 percent by weight of acrylonitrile units $(-CH_2-\underset{\underset{CN}{|}}{CH}-).$[1]

The modacrylic fibers are copolymers containing acrylonitrile and one or more additional compounds from the vinyl group.

The modacrylic fibers have many general characteristics similar to those of the acrylic fibers. For example, they have warm, pleasing hand; good drape; resiliency; and wrinkle-resistance. Since they are very heat-sensitive, they are used chiefly in blends or in fabrics that are not ironed. However, they are more flame resistant than the acrylics and are therefore being used in children's sleepwear. Modacrylic fibers have good resistance to acids and strong alkalies but tend to accumulate static electricity.

Modacrylic fibers are used in deep pile fabrics for use in linings or as the outer fabric in coats, draperies, blankets, and floor coverings.

Trademark names of modacrylic fibers are *Verel* (staple and tow, Eastman), *Dynel* (staple

[1] Except fibers qualifying under category (2) of the generic description for rubber and fibers qualifying under generic description for anidex.

and tow, Union Carbide), and *SEF* (fire-retardant staple, Monsanto).

Novoloid

Novoloid is a manufactured fiber containing at least 85 percent by weight of a cross-linked novolac.

Novoloid is a new generic group of fibers, defined by the Federal Trade Commission in a ruling that became effective as of February 15, 1974. Novoloid fibers are phenolic fibers. The first fiber in this generic group has been produced under the brand name of *Kynol*, developed by the Carborundum Company. The properties given below are based on the manufacturer's claims.

Advantages of novoloid fibers: (1) They have excellent resistance to organic solvents.

(2) The fibers resist flame temperatures to 2500°C.

(3) They are non-melting; when subjected to flame, they convert to carbon fibers and remain in fabric form to provide continued protection.

(4) They have fair resistance to dilute oxidizing acids and dilute alkalies.

Limitations of novoloid fibers: Poor resistance to concentrated oxidizing acids and to concentrated alkalies.

Nylon

Nylon is a manufactured fiber in which the fiber-forming substance is a long chain synthetic polyamide in which less than 85 percent of the amide $(-\underset{\underset{O}{||}}{C}-NH-)$ *linkages are attached directly to two aromatic rings.*

The definition of the nylon generic group was revised by the Federal Trade Commission under the rules and regulations of the Textile Fiber Products Identification Act and became effective as of January 11, 1974.

Nylon 66. Nylon 66 is produced chemically from starting materials which include benzene or phenol, hydrogen, ammonia, and caustic soda. These products are derived from coal, gas, and sea water; hence, the statement that "nylon is made from coal, water, and air." An organic base, hexamethylene diamine, and an organic

SOME NYLON FIBERS AND YARNS

Trademark Name	Description	Manufacturer*
Anso - X	Anti-static staple (carpets)	Allied Chemical
Caprolan (type 6)	Yarns, monofilaments, and textured yarns	Allied Chemical
Crepeset	Anti-static filament	American Enka
Enka (type 6)	Staple fiber and filament	American Enka
Enkalure II	Multilobal filament yarns (carpets)	American Enka
Cadon	Multilobal	Monsanto
Chemstrand (type 66)	Filament	Monsanto
Antron I, II	Trilobal Multifilament yarn	du Pont
Antron III	Anti-static filament	du Pont
Cantrece	Bicomponent fiber	du Pont
Nylon 420	Low elongation staple fiber	du Pont
Qiana	Staple, filament, textured	du Pont
Celanese (type 66)	Filament	Fiber Industries
Firestone (type 6)	Filament, textured filament	Firestone
Tajmir (nylon 4)	Staple fiber and filament	Alrac Corporation

* See Appendix for full name and address.

acid, adipic acid, derived from these materials are reacted together to form a salt. Many molecules of nylon salt are linked together under high temperatures to form a long chain of molecules known as a polymer. The nylon polymer, which is a polyamide, cools and is broken into chips. These chips are melted and extruded through a spinneret into air to harden. The resulting filaments are weak and dull in appearance. When they are cool, the filaments are stretched greatly in length in a process called cold drawing to make them stronger, finer, and more lustrous. They may be used as filaments or chopped into staple fibers.

Nylon 6. Nylon 6 differs from nylon 66 in that slightly different materials and chemical processing are used. Nylon 6 has a slightly lower melt-ing point than nylon 66. Modifications of nylon fibers have resulted in anti-cling, anti-static characteristics for wearing apparel and home furnishings.

The dyeability of nylon fibers for apparel and home furnishings has been enhanced with differential or cross-dyeing and with space-dyeing of regular, deep-dyeing, and cationic dyeable fibers.

Advantages of nylon fibers: (1) Are very strong, resilient, and elastic.

(2) Have high wet strength.

(3) Are dimensionally stable.

(4) Resist alkaline substances, mildew, and insect damage.

(5) Have excellent abrasion resistance.

(6) Can be heat-set to retain pleats.

Advantages of nylon fibers (Continued)

(7) Resist non-oily stains.

(8) Wash easily and dry quickly.

(9) Blend well with other fibers and add strength and abrasion resistance in blends.

(10) Are heat sensitive.

(11) Have low moisture absorption.

(12) May be laundered, wetcleaned, or dry-cleaned depending on dyes, finishes, design application, and garment construction.

Limitations of nylon fibers: (1) Are damaged by sunlight; bright types have better resistance to sunlight than dull types. Special additives may increase light resistance.

(2) Accumulate static electricity.

(3) Are affected by strong acid substances.

(4) Absorb and hold body oils and perspiration.

(5) May show yarn slippage in some filament yarn fabrics.

(6) Melt rather than burn, but may be flammable in sheer and brushed pile fabrics because of the finishes.

(7) Fabrics made from a staple nylon tend to pill.

(8) White nylon picks up dye and soil in laundering.

(9) White nylons require whitening with special nylon whiteners or bleaching with hydrogen peroxide, sodium perborate, or chlorine bleaches.

Nytril

Nytril is a manufactured fiber containing at least 85 percent of a long chain polymer of vinylidene dinitrile $(CH_2—C(CN)_2—)$ *where the vinylidene dinitrile content is no less than every other unit in the polymer chain.*

Darvan (Celanese), a nytril fiber, is no longer being made in the United States.

Olefin

Olefin is a manufactured fiber in which the fiber-forming substance is any long chain synthetic polymer composed of at least 85 percent by weight of ethylene, propylene, or other olefin units.[1] Most of the currently produced olefin fibers are composed of polypropylene. The olefins

are strong fibers but have comparatively low melting points. Significant developments in dyeability of olefin fibers, which previously resisted available dyes, are accelerating the use of olefin in apparel and home fashions. Both solution dyed and dyeable forms of bulked continuous yarns are available for carpet use.

An important use for olefin fabrics is in seat covers for automobiles and outdoor furniture. Other uses are in hosiery, sweaters, carpets, and cordage.

Some trademark names for olefin fibers are *DLP* (Dawbarn), *Durel* (Celanese Corporation), *Herculon* (Hercules, Incorporated), *Vectra* (Enjay Fibers and Laminates Company), and *Marvess* (Phillips Fibers Corporation).

Advantages of olefin fibers: (1) They are chemically inert to alkalies and dilute acids and are resistant to mildew.

(2) They do not absorb water readily; will float.

(3) They have high strength and high abrasion resistance.

(4) Olefin fibers can be used for special fabrics or marine cordage.

(5) They have good resilience.

(6) Heavy denier yarns are used to make three-dimensional effects in upholstery fabrics.

Limitations of olefin fibers: (1) They shrink easily when heat is applied.

(2) They have low melting points.

(3) They are affected by concentrated nitric acid and oxidizing agents.

(4) They are light-sensitive.

(5) They readily absorb mineral and vegetable oils which cause swelling of fibers.

Polyester

Polyester is a manufactured fiber in which the fiber-forming substance is any long chain synthetic polymer composed of at least 85 percent by weight of an ester of a dihydric alcohol and terephthalic acid $(p—HOOC—C_6H_4—COOH)$.

Polyester fibers are produced by the polymerization of the product formed when an alcohol and organic acid react. The product is melted and extruded through a spinneret. Then the hot or cold filaments are stretched to several times their original length. They may be used as filaments or chopped into staple.

---

[1] Except amorphous (non-crystalline) polyolefins qualifying under category (1) of the generic description for rubber.

Polyester (Continued)

The outstanding characteristic of polyesters is their ability to resist wrinkling and to spring back into shape when creased. In addition, polyesters have good dimensional stability, wash and dry easily and quickly, and possess excellent wash-and-wear or minimum-care characteristics. Modifications in polyester fiber structures have provided low-pilling polyester (Dacron 53) to be used as a blend with cotton, cross-dyeable fibers which create multicolor effects from a single dye bath and multilobal cross-sections for improved silk-like hand and drape.

One of the chief uses of polyester fibers is in apparel fabrics of the wash-and-wear, minimum-care or durable-press types. Polyesters are also used in casement curtains, throw rugs, and as a cushioning or insulating material.

Some representative polyester fibers and yarns are *Vycron* (filament, staple, tow, Beaunit), *Fortrel* (filament, staple, tow, Fiber Industries), *Dacron* (filament, staple, tow, du Pont), and *Kodel* (staple, tow, Eastman), *Trevira* (filament, staple, Hoechst).

Advantages of polyester fibers: (1) Are wrinkle-resistant and resilient.

(2) Have good dimensional stability.

(3) Wash and dry easily.

(4) Have excellent wash-and-wear characteristics.

(5) Are resistant to moths and mildew.

(6) Have high abrasion resistance.

(7) Have good strength.

(8) May be heat-set for dimensional stability and pleat-retention.

(9) Blend well with other fibers to increase wrinkle resistance.

(10) Can be laundered, wetcleaned, or drycleaned, depending on dyes, finishes, design application, and garment construction.

(11) Have good light resistance behind glass.

(12) White *Dacron* can be bleached with a chlorine-type bleach.

Limitations of polyester fibers: (1) Have poor affinity for many dyes.

(2) Are heat sensitive.

(3) Accumulate static electricity

(4) Have high affinity for oily soil and oil-borne stains.

(5) Some fabrics made from staple yarns tend to pill.

(6) Fabrics of filament yarns may show yarn slippage.

(7) Have low moisture absorption.

(8) Will burn in flame but are self-extinguishing when removed from flame.

Rayon

Rayon is a manufactured fiber composed of regenerated cellulose, as well as manufactured fibers composed of regenerated cellulose in which substituents have replaced not more than 15 percent of the hydrogens of the hydroxyl groups.

Two basic processes by which rayon is produced are viscose and cuprammonium. They are described in the sections that follow:

Viscose Rayon. Viscose rayon is produced by treating purified cellulose made from wood pulp with alkali and carbon disulfide to form a thick solution. After aging and chemical treatments, the purified cellulose xanthate solution is extruded through tiny holes in a spinneret and is solidified in a weak acid bath into regenerated cellulose filaments.

The degree of luster may be controlled by the introduction of pigments into the spinning solution. For solution-dyed yarns, the coloring components are added to the spinning solution.

The continuous filaments are stretched as they harden to increase their strength and elasticity.

To produce a smooth yarn, slight twist is added to the groups of filaments. A softer, fuzzy yarn is produced by chopping the filaments into short lengths, called staple fibers, and by carding and spinning as if the fibers were cotton or wool.

One of the major limitations of conventional yarns produced by the viscose process is their lack of dimensional stability. However, improved viscose rayons are being produced by modification of the spinning conditions.

These improved rayons are called *high wet modulus* rayons because they gain their improved dimensional stability from a greater resistance to deformation, especially when wet. They absorb slightly less water than conventional viscose rayons and swell less. They can be

SOME RAYON FIBERS AND YARNS

Trademark Name	Description	Manufacturer*
Bemberg	Cuprammonium filament	Beaunit
Cupioni	Thick-and-thin cuprammonium	Beaunit
Nub-lite	Nubby, thick-and-thin cuprammonium	Beaunit
Xena	High wet modulus	Beaunit
Enka	American Enka name for viscose products	American Enka
Jetspun	Solution-dyed viscose filament	American Enka
Zantrel or Polynosic	High wet modulus	American Enka
Avril or Fiber 40	High wet modulus	FMC
Avron	High strength staple fiber	FMC
Rayflex	High strength viscose filament	FMC
Coloray	Solution-dyed viscose staple	Courtaulds
Lirelle	High wet modulus	Courtaulds
Fibro	Viscose staple fiber	Courtaulds
Nupron	High wet modulus viscose fiber	IRC
Strawn	Straw-like rayon monofilament, bright and dull; for upholstery and drapery fabrics	IRC

*See Appendix for full name and address.

given a compressive shrinkage treatment to reduce relaxation shrinkage.

When resin treated, fabrics made from high wet modulus fibers gain crease recovery without the loss in strength that usually occurs when natural cellulosic fibers are resin treated. The high wet modulus fibers are said to be 50 percent stronger than conventional viscose fibers dry and 100 percent stronger wet.

Fabrics made from high modulus fibers can be described as having a crisp, firm hand with good drapeability and a subdued luster resembling that of silk.

Advantages of high wet modulus fibers: (1) Have moderate wet and dry strength.

(2) Have good dimensional stability.

(3) Have crisp, firm hand.

(4) Have moderate abrasion resistance.

(5) Have good drapeability.

Limitations of high wet modulus fibers: (1) Are weakened by light.

(2) Are damaged by acids.

(3) Are susceptible to mildew.

(4) Have low resiliency.

(5) Require low ironing temperatures.

(6) Have slightly lower degree of water absorption than conventional viscose rayon.

Cuprammonium Rayon (Bemberg, trademark name of Beaunit Fibers). In the cuprammonium (or Bemberg) process, cotton linters, which are short waste fibers that stick to cotton seeds, are dissolved in a copper ammonium hydroxide solution which gives the process its name. After aging, the solution is extruded into a weak acid bath where it hardens intò cellulose filaments. These filaments are immediately stretched to increase their strength and fineness.

Advantages of conventional viscose and cuprammonium fibers: (1) Are suitable for a wide range of fabrics from lightweight, luxury types to heavy, strong, durable types.

(2) Dye easily; solution-dyed yarns have high colorfastness.

(3) Blend well with other fibers.

(4) Are absorbent.

(5) Can be given many finishes.

(6) Can be laundered, wetcleaned, or dry-cleaned, depending on dye, finish, design application, and garment design.

(7) Can be bleached with chlorine-type bleaches although peroxygen type is preferable because of low initial strength.

Limitations of conventional viscose and cuprammonium fibers: (1) Are weaker when wet than when dry and have only fair abrasion resistance.

(2) Have low resiliency and poor dimensional stability.

(3) Are weakened by exposure to light, especially dull type yarns.

(4) Are susceptible to mildew.

(5) Are damaged by acid substances.

(6) Require low ironing temperatures.

Rubber Fibers

Rubber is a manufactured fiber in which the fiber-forming substance is comprised of natural or synthetic rubber, including the following categories:

(1) a manufactured fiber in which the fiber-forming substance is a hydrocarbon such as natural rubber, polyisoprene, polybutadiene, copolymers of dienes and hydrocarbons, or amorphous (non-crystalline) polyolefins.

(2) a manufactured fiber in which the fiber-forming substance is a copolymer of acrylonitrile and a diene (such as butadiene) composed of not more than 50 percent but at least 10 percent by weight of acrylonitrile units $(-CH_2-CH-)$. *The term "lastrile" may be used*
$$CN$$

as a generic description for fibers falling within this category.

(3) a manufactured fiber in which the fiber-forming substance is a polychloroprene or a copolymer of chloroprene in which at least 35 percent by weight of the fiber-forming substance is composed of chloroprene units $(-CH_2-C=CH-CH_2-)$.
$$Cl$$

Fiber-forming substances referred to in the generic description are called elastomers.

For its textile uses, rubber is extruded through a spinneret to the desired fineness. The rubber core is usually covered with one or more fibers.

Some trademark names for rubber yarns are *Lastex, Lactron,* and *Laton* of UniRoyal, Inc.

Advantages of rubber fibers: (1) They have low strength.

(2) They have exceptionally high elongation.

(3) They have moderate holding power.

(4) They can be adapted for many uses such as elastic webbings, waist bands, stitching threads for decorative effects, a variety of elastic fabrics.

Limitations of rubber fibers: (1) They are severely damaged by oils, including body oils.

(2) They are damaged by light.

(3) In some uses, flexing causes breakage of yarns and loss of elasticity.

(4) In some uses, bondings may become soft and tacky from perspiration or cleaning.

(5) Some fabrics are easily discolored in wear from perspiration; some discolor in laundering.

Saran

Saran is a manufactured fiber in which the fiber-forming substance is any long chain synthetic polymer composed of at least 80 percent by weight of vinylidene chloride units $(-CH_2-CCl_2-)$.

Saran has high resilience, low absorbency, little chemical reaction. Fibers are used for upholstery fabric, water-repellent fabrics for lawn and patio furniture, rugs, and similar constructions. They are also used in industrial fabrics.

Saran is also the generic name for a fiber made from 85 percent polyvinylidene chloride and 15 percent polyvinyl chloride. These are polymerized by heat and a catalyst. The copolymer is melted, extruded into cool air, then quenched.

The filaments are cold-drawn in the same manner as nylon.

Saran by Enjay (Enjay Fibers and Laminates Company) and *Lus-Trus* (Southern Lus-Trus Corporation) are tradenames of saran fibers.

Advantages of saran fibers: (1) Are highly resilient.

(2) Are very resistant to acid and alkaline substances.

(3) Are resistant to staining.

(4) Are flame-resistant; do not support combustion.

(5) Resist moisture, weather, moths, mildew.

(6) Have good abrasion resistance.

(7) May be wetcleaned or drycleaned depending on construction of item.

(8) White fabrics may be bleached with chlorine-type bleach in bath not above 100°F.

Limitations of saran fibers: (1) Tend to retain wrinkles; fabrics should be air-dried.

(2) Cannot be pressed because steam causes excessive shrinkage.

(3) Are heat sensitive.

(4) Fabrics tend to shrink in synthetic solvents due to swelling action.

(5) Have little chemical reaction.

(6) Have low moisture absorbency.

(7) Solution-dyed fabrics have good colorfastness to light but are limited in range of colors.

Spandex

Spandex is a manufactured fiber in which the fiber-forming substance is a long chain synthetic polymer comprised of at least 85 percent of a segmented polyurethane.

Yarns made of this man-made elastomer are used where good holding power combined with softness and light weight are desired. The fiber can be made into a filament yarn to be used uncovered or covered with another textile fiber. The yarns are used in foundation garments, swimwear, surgical hose, and other elastic products. Core-spun spandex yarns are being used to produce stretch garments.

Trademark names include *Lycra* (du Pont), *Numa* (American Cyanamid Company), *Vyrene* (UniRoyal, Inc.), *Glospan* (Globe Manufacturing Company), *Fulflex* (Carr-Fulflex, Inc.), *Unel* (Union Carbide).

Advantages of spandex fibers: (1) They are more resistant than rubber to perspiration, body oils, cosmetic oils, oxidation, and drycleaning damage.

(2) They are more light resilient than rubber but may yellow on exposure to light.

Limitations of spandex fibers: Some spandex fibers should not be bleached with chlorine bleaches; others are more resistant.

Vinal

Vinal is a manufactured fiber in which the fiber-forming substance is any long chain synthetic polymer composed of at least 50 percent by weight of vinyl alcohol units ($-CH_2-CHOH-$), and in which the total of the vinyl alcohol units and any one or more of the various acetal units is at least 85 percent by weight of the fiber.

Vinal is not currently produced in the United States.

Vinyon

Vinyon is a manufactured fiber in which the fiber-forming substance is any long chain synthetic polymer composed of at least 85 percent by weight of vinyl chloride units ($-CH_2-CHCl-$).

These substances are polymerized into larger molecules by heating in the presence of a catalyst. The vinyon is then dissolved in acetone and extruded into warm air. The filaments are cold-drawn.

Avisco Vinyon HH (FMC Corporation) is a trademark name for vinyon staple fiber.

Advantages of vinyon fiber: (1) It has high resistance to acids and alkalies.

(2) It is resistant to water, hence has built-in water-repellency.

(3) Vinyon fiber does not burn although it does melt.

(4) Vinyon is a strong, very elastic fiber.

(5) Vinyon fiber is easily heat-bonded to other fibers.

Limitations of vinyon fiber: (1) It is dissolved by many solvents.

(2) Vinyon melts at a very low temperature; shrinks when heated above 150°F.

(3) It is affected by trichlorethylene, acetone, chloroform, pyrodene, ethyl acetate, amyl acetate, toluol, and benzol.

IDENTIFICATION CHARACTERISTICS OF NATURAL FIBERS

Generic Name	Trade Name	Microscopic Appearance	Burning	Methods of Testing Solvent	Staining*	Density Group
Cotton	—		ODOR OF BURNING PAPER	*70 percent sulfuric acid* Insol. conc. HCl distinguishes from rayons (1)	*Unstained by zinc chloride iodine (2)*	1.45-1.6
Silk	—		ODOR OF BURNING FEATHERS	*8.9 N hydrochloric acid*	None characteristic	1.2-1.28
Wool	—		ODOR OF BURNING FEATHERS	*Boiling 5 percent NaOH*	None characteristic	1.28-1.35

*Other than general dye stain.

Note: The first method for identifying a fiber is printed in capital letters; confirming reactions are printed in italics. For those fibers that have several confirming reactions, the numbers in parentheses show the order in which the easiest and more certain confirmations may be obtained.

IDENTIFICATION CHARACTERISTICS OF MAN-MADE FIBERS

Generic Name	Trade Name	Microscopic Appearance †	Burning	Methods of Testing Solvent	Staining*	Density Group
Acetate	—		Melts and burns**	80 PERCENT ACETONE	None characteristic	1.28-1.35
Acrylic	Acrilan		Melts and burns**	DIMETHYL FORMAMIDE at 100°C; Insoluble in 2.5:1 nitric acid distinguishes from Creslan	Blue with Anthraquinone Blue SWF distinguishes from Orlon; Pink with Fastusol Pink BBA distinguishes from Zefran and Creslan	1.1-1.2
Acrylic	Creslan		Melts and burns**	DIMETHYL FORMAMIDE 2.5-1 nitric acid	None characteristic	1.1-1.2
Acrylic	Orlon 42		Melts and burns**	DIMETHYL FORMAMIDE, ROOM TEMP.	Unstained by Anthraquinone Blue SWF	1.1-1.2
Acrylic	Zefran		Melts and burns**	DIMETHYL FORMAMIDE at 100°C	Stained red with Fastusol Pink BBA	1.1-1.2
Glass	—		DOES NOT BURN	Hydrofluoric acid	None	2.56
Modacrylic	Dynel		Self-extinguishes until charred; then burns readily	HOT 100 PERCENT ACETONE (Caution: low flash point)	Stains blue green with Anthraquinone Blue SWF distinguishes from Verel	1.28-1.35

NOTE: See footnotes at end of chart, page 28.

IDENTIFICATION CHARACTERISTICS OF MAN-MADE FIBERS (Cont.)

Generic Name	Trade Name	Microscopic Appearance†	Burning	Methods of Testing Solvent	Staining*	Density Group
Modacrylic	Verel	Distinguishes from Dynel (2)	Melts and burns; odor of cordite	HOT 100 PERCENT ACETONE	Stains pale blue with Anthraquinone Blue SWF; distinguishes from Dynel (1)	1.37
Nylon 6	—		Melts and burns; odor of celery	4.2 N HYDROCHLORIC ACID	Stains darker than nylon 66	1.1-1.2
Nylon 66			Melts and burns; odor of celery	1:1 HYDROCHLORIC ACID FORMIC ACID 88 percent phenol	Stains lighter than nylon 6	1.1-1.2
Olefin (Polyethylene)	—		Melts and burns; odor of burning paraffin	HOT CYCLOHEXANE	None characteristic	0.95
Olefin (Polypropylene)	—		Melts and burns; faint odor of asphalt	HOT DECALIN	None characteristic	0.9
Polyester	Dacron		Melts and burns**	DIMETHYL FORMAMIDE at 140°C; fans in 88 percent phenol	Unstained with alcoholic Anthraquinone Blue SWF; Dacron 64 stains deeper shades with dye stains	1.35-1.45
Polyester	Kodel		Melts and burns**	METHYL SALICYLATE AT BOIL; does not fan in 88 percent phenol (dependent on type)	None characteristic	1.2-1.38

Fiber	Trade name	Burning	Solubility	Staining	Refractive index
Rayon (Cuprammonium)	Bemberg	ODOR OF BURNING PAPER	Conc. hydrochloric acid	Deep blue with Brilliant Benzo Blue 6BA distinguishes from viscose and Fortisans	1.45-1.6
Rayon (Saponified acetate)	Fortisan	ODOR OF BURNING PAPER	Slowly soluble in conc. HCl	Unstained with Anthraquinone Blue SWF and Brilliant Benzo Blue 6BA distinguishes from viscose and cuprammonium	1.45-1.6
Rayon (Viscose process)	Jetspun	ODOR OF BURNING PAPER	Conc. hydrochloric acid	Unstained by Brilliant Benzo Blue 6BA, tinted blue with Anthraquinone Blue SWF distinguishes from cuprammonium and Fortisans	1.45-1.6
Saran	—	Melts and burns	TETRAHYDROFURAN	None characteristic	1.7
Triacetate	Arnel	Melts and burns**	METHYLENE CHLORIDE/ETHANOL; insol. 80 percent acetone distinguishes from acetate	None characteristic	1.28-1.35

NOTE: See footnotes at end of chart, page 28.

IDENTIFICATION CHARACTERISTICS OF MAN-MADE FIBERS (Cont.)

Generic Name	Trade Name	Microscopic Appearance†	Burning	Methods of Testing Solvent	Staining*	Density Group
Vinal (Produced in Japan)	Kuralon		Melts and burns**	1:1 HYDROCHLORIC ACID; insol. 88 percent phenol distinguishes from nylons (1)	None	1.28-1.35 distinguishes from nylon (2)
Vinyon	Avisco Vinyon HH		Melts and burns**	CHLOROFORM INSOL. ACETIC ACID	None characteristic	1.28-1.35

†Other cross sections are possible for many of the man-made fibers. For example, the cross section of Antron nylon is trilobal rather than round as is the case with regular nylon.
*Other than general dye stain.
**Burning test for these fibers is not definitive.

Note: The following table gives the information available on some of the newer fibers, listed here under generic names.

	Anidex	Aramid	Metallic	Novoloid	Spandex
Specific Gravity	1.22	1.38-1.44	7.9	1.25	1.2-1.25
Burning	Chars and degrades above 851°F.	Very slow to ignite; has high melting point	Burns slowly with melting	DOES NOT BURN	Burns and melts; leaves fluffy residue
Solubility	60 percent sulfuric acid	100 percent sulfuric acid	May corrode but otherwise generally resists chemical action	70 percent nitric acid or 50 percent sodium hydroxide (Boiled 100 hours)	Dimethylformamide

SUMMARY CHART ON TEXTILE FIBERS

Fiber	Chief Apparel and Household Uses	Characteristics	Precautions
		NATURAL FIBERS	
Cotton	Light- and medium-weight apparel Household textiles	Versatile Durable Can withstand frequent hard laundering Is easily ironed at high temperatures	Protect stored items against dampness to prevent mildew
Linen	Women's and children's blouses and dresses; summer suiting Handkerchiefs Table linens Other household fabrics	Beauty and luster endure through frequent hard launderings Does not shed lint May be more expensive than cotton Wrinkles easily unless treated to resist wrinkling Resistant to dye-type stains	For best wear, do not press in sharp creases Protect stored items against dampness to prevent mildew For smooth appearance, iron at high temperature
Silk	Light- and medium-weight apparel Accessory items such as scarfs Some expensive upholstery and drapery fabrics	Has natural luster and strength Is moderately resilient to wrinkles and readily returns to shape Dyes well Is more expensive than man-made (filament) silky yarns Some items may be carefully hand-laundered	To clean most items, dryclean Protect from prolonged exposure to light Protect against moths and carpet beetles
Wool	Outerwear Light-, medium-, or heavy-weight apparel Blankets Carpets Upholstery	Springs back into shape; requires little pressing Has great versatility in fabrics and colors Has insulating capacity which increases with fabric thickness; hence fabric can be warm or cold.	Dryclean most items Never wash woolens in hot water. Moist heat and agitation as in some laundering will shrink and felt wool Protect against moths and carpet beetles

SUMMARY CHART ON TEXTILE FIBERS

Fiber	Chief Apparel and Household Uses	Characteristics	Precautions
MAN-MADE FIBERS			
Acetate	Light- and medium-weight apparel Drapery and upholstery fabrics Fiberfill	Drapes well Dries quickly Is inexpensive Is subject to fume-fading Has poor abrasion resistance Loses some strength when wet	Iron or press only at very low temperature to prevent melting and fusing of fibers

*Acrylic
  Acrilan
  Creslan
  Orlon
  Zefran
  Zefkrome
	Tailored outerwear
	Knitted wear
	Pile fabrics
	Blankets
	Carpets
		Resists wrinkling and effects of sunlight
		Has high bulking power and soft hand
		Some fabrics have silky texture
			Remove oily stains before washing; waterborne stains will come out easily

Anidex
  (new fiber)
  Anim/8
	Proposed for upholstery and other household fabrics; also for wearing apparel	Has high degree of stretch and recovery
		Stays resilient through repeated washings and drycleanings
		Can be chlorine-bleached
			Launder or dryclean, according to recommendations on hang tag or care labels

*Aramid Nomex	Clothing and household goods	High temperature resistance	Precautions, if any, are not currently established
Kevlar	Tires		

*Modacrylic
  Dynel
  Verel
  Elura
  SEF
	Deep pile and fleece fabrics
	Carpets (in combination with acrylic)
		Resists wrinkling
		Resists chemicals
		Is soft and resilient and non-combustible
			Iron at extremely low temperatures only

Novoloid Kynol	Blankets, draperies Fireproof clothing and fabrics	Outstanding flame resistance Non-melting	Precautions, if any, are not currently established

SUMMARY CHART ON TEXTILE FIBERS

Fiber	Chief Apparel and Household Uses	Characteristics	Precautions
*Nylon	Hosiery, lingerie Sweaters, wind jackets dresses Carpets	Has exceptional strength and excellent elasticity Retains permanent shape Woven fabrics are often hot and uncomfortable to wear Washes easily but tends to attract dirt High abrasion resistance	Remove oily stains before washing To maintain whiteness, use any nylon whiteners on the market Press at low temperature
*Olefin *Herculon* *Marvess* *Polycrest*	Seat covers for autos, outdoor furniture Carpets	Has no water absorption Has low melting temperature	
*Polyester *Dacron* *Fortrel* *Kodel* *Vycron* *Anavor* *Avlin* *Blue C* *Encron* *Quintess* *Textura* *Trevira*	Wash-and-wear apparel, often in combination with other fibers Curtains Fiberfill	Has exceptional wrinkle resistance; therefore, needs little ironing or pressing Easy to wash Has sharp pleat and crease retention Some fabrics resist pilling	Remove oily stains before washing Follow directions given on hang tags or care labels to keep white fabrics white
Rayon (conventional)	Light- and medium-weight clothing Drapery and upholstery	Absorbent Inexpensive Moderately durable Lacks resilience; wrinkles easily Brushed or napped fabrics may be combustible	Launder carefully to prevent shrinkage or stretching: rayon does not withstand treatment that can be given cotton or linen When in doubt about the washability of garments, dryclean

SUMMARY CHART ON TEXTILE FIBERS

Fiber	Chief Apparel and Household Uses	Characteristics	Precautions
Rayon (high wet modules) *Avril* *Nupron* *Xena* *Zantrel*	Sweaters, wind jackets Dresses Home furnishings Sportswear	Can be mercerized Has higher dry and wet strength than conventional rayon Can be washed	
Rubber *Lastex*	Foundation garments Swimwear	High degree of stretch and recovery Damaged by oils and light	Wash frequently with mild soap and detergent Avoid constant overstretching
*Saran *Rovana* *Saran*	Seat covers for autos, outdoor furniture Screening, awnings Luggage	Resists soiling and staining Resists weathering Is flame resistant but sensitive to heat	To remove stains, first blot stain; then rinse with clear water
Spandex *Glospan* *Lycra* *Numa*	Foundation garments Swimwear Surgical hose Ski pants, other sportswear	Has high degree of stretch and recovery Resists abrasion Is resistant to body oils	To machine launder, use warm water and dry on lowest heat with shortest cycle
*Vinyon	Mixed with other fibers for heat bonding	Resistant to chemicals and sunlight Noncombustible	

*In addition to specific characteristics mentioned for each fiber, those fibers marked with an * have these general properties in common: (1) moderate to high strength and resilience; (2) resistance to moths and mildew; (3) sensitivity to heat of pressing iron; (4) dimensional stability; (5) resistance to shrinking or stretching; (6) tendency to accumulate static electricity in cold, dry weather; (7) non-absorbency; (8) good washing and drying qualities; (9) resistance to non-oily stains but retention of body oils that penetrate the fiber and are hard to remove; and (10) pleat retention because of thermoplastic qualities.

Paper in Textile Uses [1]

To a certain extent, paper is used for textile products. Some of these uses are:

Knit Paper Fabrics

A specially treated high-strength paper yarn is knitted into a variety of knit and mesh constructions for use in wearing apparel and household items. Paper knits are claimed to be pliable; cleanable; sewable on a regular-needle, power, trade machine; and wrinkle-resistant. They maintain shape, can be reshaped when damp, and can be pressed. They do not lose strength when wet. They are drycleanable.

Nonwoven Paper Products

A nonwoven is defined as a construction of fibers held together either chemically or mechanically. Nonwoven paper products are also known as disposables. They can be produced faster and more economically than woven or knitted fabrics made of natural or man-made fibers but must be replaced more frequently and therefore are not necessarily more economical to the consumer in the long run. Disposables do offer convenience since they need no laundering nor maintenance. Industry and institutions provide the largest markets for disposables.

Among the consumer items are tablecloths, napkins, sleeping bag liners, bedsheets, pillow cases, polishing cloths, diapers, baby bibs,

dresses, aprons, handkerchiefs, underwear, swim wear, graduation gowns.

Items for institutional use include hospital gowns for surgeons, assistants, nurses, anesthetists, laboratory technicians; also isolation gowns and x-ray caps and gowns, head covers, face masks, gloves, operating room pack, mattress covers, bed sheets, draw sheets, drop sheets, pillow cases, head rest covers, bath mats, wash cloths, hand and face towels.

Industrial uses include factory aprons, protective coveralls, work shirts and pants, industrial wipers.

A Woven Paper Product

This product, called *Papertex*, was first shown in 1955 at the World Trade Fair. It is a lightweight nylon web, coated with chemically bonded acrylic resin. It was developed by Snia Viscosa of Milan, Italy, for sportswear and accessories.

Fiber Identification

Accurate identification of fibers requires precise tests and often more than one type of test. The five methods used by textile technologists to identify fibers are: (1) burning test, (2) determination of fiber density, (3) microscopic examination, cross-section and longitudinal, (4) staining of fibers by dyes or reagents, and (5) solubility of fibers in various reagents.

The accompanying chart from the *Man-Made Textile Encyclopedia* (Textile Book Publishers, Inc., 1959) adapted with permission from pages 159-162, presents the characteristics of fibers for each of the five tests. See *Note* on chart for further explanation of tests.

---

[1] For information about producers and suppliers, write to Disposable Association, 260 Madison Avenue, New York, New York.

Yarns

All fabrics—except plastics and fabrics that are formed by the direct interlocking of fibers—depend upon the use of yarns. A *yarn* is an assemblage of fibers that are laid or twisted together to form a continuous strand. Yarns may be made from either *staple* fibers (fibers short enough to be measured in inches or centimeters) or *filament* fibers (fibers long enough to be measured in yards or meters).

Staple fibers are *spun* or *twisted* into yarns; filament fibers need little or no twist to hold them together in yarns. The type and length of fiber, the type, ply, and size of yarns, and the amount of twist given to yarns determine many of the characteristics of fabrics made from the yarns. Some fabrics, by their general appearance and properties, indicate the presence of one or more of these yarn characteristics. For example, fabrics constructed of spun yarns are less smooth than fabrics constructed of filament yarns. They also have a lower luster. Cord or rib fabrics contain ply or larger yarns in the rib direction.

Yarns may be classified by the direction and degree of twist, the form of the raw material, the number and similarity of parts, the texture or effect produced, the size, fiber content, and use.

Yarns Classified by Degree and Amount of Twist

Twist in yarns brings the fibers closer together and makes them more compact. Twist is necessary in order to make yarns from staple fibers. In contrast, fabrics can be made from filament yarns which have no twist.

The amount or *degree of twist* is expressed by the intended end-use of the yarn or in a more technical way as the number of turns per inch, expressed as the "tpi." As the degree of twist is increased, the yarn becomes harder, its luster decreases, its strength increases up to a certain point of twist, and it becomes shorter in length.

Yarns of very high twist are used to create the crinkle in true crepe fabrics. Yarns of very low twist are used in fabrics to be napped.

The characteristics of a finished fabric may be determined in part by the direction of twist, described as S-twist or Z-twist. A yarn has an S-twist if the spirals formed by the twist conform to the slope of the central part of the letter S when the yarn is held in a vertical position. A yarn has a Z-twist if the spirals conform to the central part of the letter Z. The Z-twist is the standard twist used. S-twist is used for specialized purposes and also for yarns such as ply yarns in which a reversal of direction is desired.

Yarns Classified by Form of Raw Material

Yarns Made from Staple Fibers

Yarns spun from staple fibers are normally spun by one of three conventional systems or by some non-conventional systems developed to achieve a simple, efficient, and economical spinning process.

The processes involved in each of the *conventional systems* (cotton, woolen, and worsted) are similar, but the equipment used in each system is highly specialized to deal with the length, cohesiveness, diameter, elasticity, and surface contour of the natural fiber for which it was originally designed. The resulting yarns consequently differ in characteristics, not only because of basic fiber differences but also because of differences in the total spinning system. Yarns spun by the same system will have similarities no matter what fiber is used. In each of the conventional spinning systems the processes are designed to (1) clean and parallel staple fibers, (2) draw fibers into a fine strand, and (3) twist fibers to keep them together and to give them strength.

Cotton System. Inasmuch as the cotton system of spinning is basic, an understanding of this system gives a structure upon which to compare and relate the other systems.

The first steps in the manufacture of yarns by the cotton system are the *opening* and *loosening* of the fibers in the mass as purchased, regardless of whether the fibers are natural or made-made. Leaves and other impurities are removed from cotton in a *cleaning process*. The spread-out mass of fibers is known as the *lap*.

The next step is *carding*, in which fibers are carried between large revolving drums covered with steel wire needles. This operation separates the fibers, and also removes impurities and short cotton fibers. The fibers are laid essentially in one direction in a thin web which is condensed into a soft, fluffy strand called a sliver.

Several slivers are combined for evenness and are drawn out in length to produce slivers of the desired weight. Slivers of differing fiber contents may be combined. Drawing and combining slivers blends the fibers.

The next process, *drafting* or *roving*, continues the drawing out and adds just enough twist to hold the fibers together. The actual yarn is then produced in the spinning process in which additional twist is inserted to make it strong.

Carded cotton yarns are made by the system described above. These yarns do not produce fabrics as smooth or as lustrous-looking as fabrics made from combed cotton yarns. However, fabrics made from carded cotton may be very durable. Examples of fabrics made with carded yarn are: calico, muslin, crash, cretonne, and some ginghams, chambrays, and broadcloth.

Combed cotton yarns, as the name implies, result from a *combing process*. When long staple fibers are spun in the cotton system, the carding and drawing processes are followed by a combing process which causes the fibers to be laid parallel and removes short fibers. The combed yarns consequently tend to be longer and more uniform than carded yarns. Fabrics made from combed yarns are more lustrous and smoother than fabrics made from carded yarns. Examples include: organdy, lawn, ginghams, chambrays, and broadcloth.

An advantage of the cotton system is its ability to spin finer and shorter staple fibers than the woolen and worsted systems permit. The yarns are frequently fine and the fabrics light in weight although many heavy, coarse yarn fabrics do exist. When man-made fibers are spun with cotton equipment, fiber-cut staple with length and fineness comparable to cotton is used. Blends of cotton and a man-made fiber, or 100 percent man-made fiber yarns may be made. Silk noil or waste silk may also be cut into suitable length and spun by use of this system.

Woolen System. The steps in the production of yarns by the woolen system are similar to those of the cotton system that produces cotton carded yarns. The equipment handles the shorter wool fibers and man-made fibers of similar length and coarseness. The resultant yarn is classified as a *woolen yarn*. Woolen yarns are made from fibers that are carded but not laid completely parallel or tightly twisted. This process produces a fuzzy yarn used for fabrics that are relatively soft and have a somewhat fuzzy surface. Flannel is an example of such a fabric.

Worsted System. The basic steps in the production of yarns by the worsted system are similar to those for the manufacture of combed cotton yarns. The three basic worsted systems, *French, Bradford,* and *American,* vary according to the length of fiber used, the nature of the combing process, and the actual number of steps in the process. In each system, the fibers are longer than those of the woolen system and are combed so that the fibers are comparatively parallel. In the spinning step, the yarn is given a tight twist. The resultant fabrics are comparatively smooth, have a crisp feel, and are usually tightly woven. Examples: gabardine, serge, and fabrics labeled worsted.

Non-conventional Spinning Systems. Through research, efforts are continually made to simplify yarn spinning by the elimination of some of the conventional steps. Thus far, results tend to produce a new type of yarn not comparable to yarns produced by conventional methods.

The *open-end method* introduces the drawn sliver of fibers into a rotating machine which twists and binds them to a seed yarn. This system is faster and less costly than conventional methods and produces a medium to coarse Z-twist yarn.

Twistless spinning is a method in which the roving is wetted, given a minimum twist, and spray-starched. The starch is gelatinized to give fiber bonding. The resultant yarns are soft, lustrous, flat, and ribbon-like and have good covering power for use where opaqueness is highly desirable.

Yarns Made from Filament Fibers

Silk in filament form is a fine, smooth fiber many yards long. These filaments are twisted together to form yarns. The yarns may have a high amount of twist (crepe-type yarns) or they may have no twist. Fabrics made from filament yarns are smooth and even. They may be heavy or light in weight, and may be transparent or opaque.

In much the same way as silk filaments, man-made fibers may be manufactured into filaments and then into yarns. The resulting fabrics may be similar to those described for silk or they may reflect properties unique to the man-made filaments. The degree of luster in man-made fibers can be controlled from very low to very bright. Multifilament yarns are those which are made from more than one filament. Monofilament is a single filament which may be formed into various sizes depending upon the size of the spinnerette hole and the end-use.

Yarns Made from Tow (Direct Spinning)

In addition to selling fiber in staple and filament form, man-made fiber producers sell fiber as *tow*, a thick rope of thousands of parallel filaments. Filament tow can be made into yarns without disrupting the continuity of the strand. The filaments are cut into staple of equal or variable lengths and then made into sliver (tow to top system) or yarns (tow to yarn system) in steps similar to those of the cotton system. The processing eliminates ·basic steps in the conventional systems, produces yarns that have a higher degree of strength and greater uniformity, and offers unlimited possibility for novelty effects. These qualities are best suited to upholstery fabrics. The processing can lead directly into the formation of hi-bulk yarns used in the knit apparel trade.

Yarns Classified by Number of Parts

Single Yarns

Single yarns are made from single filaments or from a group of staple or filament fibers twisted together sufficiently to form the desired yarn. A *monofilament* yarn is one made from a single filament. *Multifilament* yarns are made from more than one filament twisted together. *Spun* yarns are made from staple fibers twisted together.

Ply Yarns

Ply yarns are made by twisting together two or more single yarns. Each part of the yarn is called a ply. The number of plies used (two plies, three plies, etc.) describes the structure. Most ply yarns are twisted in the opposite direction to the twist of the singles from which they are made. Ply yarns are stronger than their equivalent single yarns of the same diameter and fiber.

Cord Yarns

Cord yarns are ply yarns twisted together. This is the structure of rope and of some types of sewing thread. Cord yarns are seldom used in conventional fabrics.

Yarns Classified by Similarity of Parts

Simple Yarns

All parts of a simple yarn are alike. A simple yarn may be a single, ply, or cord yarn of any size or fiber content. The kind and amount of texture that a simple yarn produces in a fabric depends on the texture of the yarn and the manner in which the yarn parts have been combined.

Novelty Yarns

A novelty yarn is composed of unlike parts which are irregular at regular intervals. Novelty yarns are usually ply yarns produced to give an effect or texture to a fabric rather than strength. The typical novelty yarn has three basic parts or plies, each different in structure. The basic parts, however, may be made of the same or different fibers. The central *core* or *foundation ply* is surrounded by the *fancy* or *effect ply* which is held in place by a *binder ply*.

Yarns Classified by Size

Staple Fiber Yarns

The size of spun yarns or yarns made from staple fibers is referred to as *count* or *number* and is based on a relationship of length to weight.

It is an inverse system in which the largest number designates the finest yarn and the lowest number the heaviest yarn. Specifics of the ratio will vary with the kind of fiber used. In the cotton system, the yarn number size is the number of hanks (one hank is 840 yards) required to weigh one pound. For example:

Weight and Length	Yarn Number
1 hank or 840 yards, weighing 1 pound	No. 1 yarn or 1^s
10 hanks or 8400 yards, weighing 1 pound	No. 10 yarn or 10^s

The woolen and worsted systems also follow indirect numbering but differ in yardage per hank according to the system used.

Filament Fiber Yarns

The size of yarns made from man-made or silk filaments is expressed as *denier*. Denier is defined as the weight in grams of 9000 meters of yarn. It is a direct system based on the weight per length of yarn. The higher the denier number, the coarser the yarn. In man-made filaments the size can be controlled by the size of the holes in the spinnerette and the rate of flow of the solution through the spinnerette. Denier is also used to express the size of the filaments before formation into yarns. Both the size of the basic filament and the number of filaments within the yarn combine to determine the denier of a yarn.

Yarns Classified by Method of Producing Texture

Yarns used to create other than comparatively smooth textures in fabrics may be achieved by (1) modifications in the spinning process of simple yarns to create irregularities of texture, (2) combining these modified or effect yarns with a core and binder to create a novelty yarn, (3) modifying a thermoplastic fiber by mechanical texturizing methods, or (4) using bicomponent fibers in making the yarn.

Modification in Spinning Process of Simple Yarns

Variations in texture that result from modifications in the spinning process of simple yarns used singly or as the novelty part of novelty yarns are identified by such terms as:

Bouclé Yarns. Bouclé is one of the most used novelty yarns. It is characterized by an effect yarn forming tight loops which project from the body of the yarn at fairly regular intervals. These yarns are often made of a combination of fibers. They are used in knitted or woven fabrics.

Loop or Curl Yarns. These yarns have They may be used in woven or knitted fabrics to create a looped pile such as astrakhan, and for textured effects on other types of coating and dress fabrics.

Nub Yarns. A nub yarn is formed by twisting one yarn around another many times within a short space to create enlarged places on the surface of the base yarn. Sometimes a binder is used to hold the nub in place. These nubs may be uniformly spaced on the base yarn or they may be irregularly spaced. This type yarn is also called *knot, spot,* or *knop* yarn.

Ratiné Yarns. A ratiné yarn is very similar to a bouclé yarn. In ratiné the loops are twisted continuously and are not spaced as they are in bouclé.

Seed Yarns. Seed yarns are similar to nub yarns, although the nub is very small. These yarns often use a natural fiber for the core or base yarn and a man-made fiber for the applied seed.

Slub Yarns. True slub yarns are made by varying the tension of yarn twist at regular intervals to produce soft, thick elongated low twist areas (slubs). A core or binder yarn may or may not be used. On fabrics such as shantung and slub broadcloth, the slub in these yarns can be seen.

Snarl Yarns. A snarl yarn is made by twisting at one time two or more yarns held at different tension. The effect yarn forms alternating unclosed loops along both sides of the core yarn.

Spiral or Corkscrew Yarns. A spiral yarn is made by twisting together two yarns of different thickness and twist, one soft and heavy and the other fine. The heavy yarn is fed faster than the fine yarn and winds around it in a spiral formation.

SOME EXAMPLES OF TEXTURED YARNS

Trademark Name	Fiber	Texturing Method and Description*
Agilon (Deering Milliken)	Nylon, *Dacron* Polyester	Edge crimping process *Stretch; no-torque type*
Cadon (Monsanto)	Nylon	*Second generation bulk yarn (for carpets)*
Cumuloft (Monsanto)	Nylon	*Bulk yarn*
Encron (American Enka)	Polyester	Heat-set under false twist
Fluflon **	Nylon, *Dacron*	Heat-set under false twist *Stretch yarn; false-twist type*
Helanca (Heberlein)	Nylon, *Dacron*	False twist *Several types: stretch yarn, conventional type; no torque and modified type*
Monvelle (Monsanto)	Nylon, Spandex	Conjugate spun, i.e., nylon and spandex segments extruded side by side and joined entire length *Stretch yarn*
Saaba**	Nylon, *Dacron*	False-twist type stretch yarn modified to remove some of the stretch, retain maximum bulk, and control surface texture *Stretch yarn, modified type*
Superloft **	Nylon, *Dacron, Orlon, Arnel*	Heat-set under false twist *Stretch yarn, false-twist type, filament*
Taslan (J. P. Stevens)	Fiberglas, Rayon, Polyester	Air jet; yarn structure is opened, loops formed, and structure closed again *Bulk yarn, loop type*

* Note that the description of each yarn is given in italics.

** Trademark name of a type of textured yarn produced on Leesona Corporation machinery.

Modification of Thermoplastic Filament Yarns

Variations in texture that result from the application of heat to a thermoplastic continuous filament yarn so as to displace the compact position of the filaments and produce a crimp, coil, curl, or loop can be classified as bulk, stretch, or modified stretch yarns. They are commonly referred to as *textured yarns*.

The texturing process increases the surface area of the yarn, allowing more circulation of air through the fabric, greater moisture absorption, and higher thermal insulation. The yarns gain in bulk and resiliency without gaining weight. The resultant yarn has many of the desirable characteristics of spun yarns without the pilling and shedding of spun yarns or the cost of converting man-made filaments to staple fibers.

In greatly simplified terms, the procedures used to form the textured yarns are: filament is removed from the bobbins; individual filaments are released and their usual positions changed in some manner (for example, twisting); the filaments are heat-set in the desired configuration then untwisted.

Bulk Textured Yarns. The bulk-type texturing processes can be used with any type of filament fiber. Filaments may be fluffed, crimped, or curled by (1) passing the yarn through gear-teeth rollers, or (2) packing or stuffing the yarn into a stuffer box and heat-setting the yarn in a crimped position, or (3) subjecting the yarn to the pressure of an air jet. In each case heat is applied simultaneously.

These processes can increase bulk from 100 to 300 percent but give only a minimal amount of stretch or elasticity. They are used as carpet yarns, in tricot fabrication, in sweater fabrics, and for novelty textures. The resultant fabrics are usually soft and opaque with some degree of bulk and warmth but are light in weight.

Stretch Textured Yarns. The stretch-type texturing processes given to thermoplastic fibers produce coiled or crimped yarns of 300 to 500 percent elongation. Two basic techniques are used: In the *false-twist method*, the yarn is twisted, heat-set, and untwisted. This process results in a coiled yarn which will expand when pulled. In the *edge-crimp method*, the heat filaments are drawn over a knifelike edge which flattens one side and causes the yarn to curl. Both methods impart a permanent *torque* or *twist* to a thermoplastic yarn. This yarn is expandable when stretched and may be used in fabrics for garments that require a form-fitting resilience without pressure. Stretch yarns are distinguished from elastic yarns based on rubber and other elastomers in that the stretch of elastic yarns is a basic polymer property not associated with yarn curl.

Modified Stretch Yarns. These are also known as textured "set" yarns. They are made in basically the same manner as stretch textured yarns except for a final step of stabilizing or setting the yarn by heat after the untwisting step. Although the yarn is stabilized it still tends to return to its twisted shape. Modified stretch yarns are characterized by bulk, loftiness, and about 10 to 15 percent of stretch. They lack the recovery characteristic of regular stretch yarns but are effectively used in polyester doubleknits and in textured fabrics woven of man-made fibers when texture, wrinkle resistance, and ease of care are desired.

Yarns Made from Bicomponent Fibers

Bicomponent fibers are composed of two generically similar but chemically or physically different polymers joined physically in a single filament. The components can be joined side by side or bilaterally or in a sheath-core structure in which one component forms the sheath and the other the core.

Due to the chemical differences of the components each shrinks to a different degree when exposed to certain conditions such as heat or moisture. The difference in shrinkage causes a pulling of the yarn into a crimped conformation creating bulk and texture. Typical bicomponent yarns are *Orlon* and *Sayella* used in sweaters and *Nylon Cantrece II* used for close-fitting and resilient hosiery.

Yarns Classified by Fiber Content

Yarns may be made entirely of one fiber (man-made or natural) and be classified as such by the name of the fiber used. Or yarns may be a blend of two or more fibers the names of which are included in the description of the yarn. Yarns are blended to capitalize on the good qualities of a fiber and to minimize its weaker qualities by the combining of fibers that complement each other in the desirable characteristics they provide.

Blends and Combinations

Blended Yarns. Yarns may be combined or blended in any of these ways: (1) by mixing staple fibers before they are spun; (2) by combining filament fibers before adding twist; (3) by combining simple yarns of different fiber content into a ply yarn. A combination can also be achieved by blending two generically different polymers before they are spun. In this latter process, a solution does not form, but one polymer becomes the matrix surrounded by fibrils formed by the other polymer. The result is known as a biconstituent fiber. The primary goal achieved is similar to the purpose of the mechanical mixing of staple or filament fiber.

Fabrics of more than one fiber content are described in terms of the manner in which the combination was achieved.

Blended fabrics are those made of yarns in which two or more fibers are mixed before the yarn is spun. These yarns may be used as either warp or filling or may be used in both directions.

Combination fabrics contain yarns of different fibers. Warp and filling may be of different fibers, each color of yarn in yarn-dyed fabrics may be a different fiber, or each ply of a ply or novelty yarn may be a different fiber.

More simply, in a "blend," fibers are mixed before spinning, and in a "combination," fibers are mixed in weaving or during plying of the yarn.

Blends may be made for economic, aesthetic, or functional purposes, or they may be used to facilitate one of the manufacturing processes.

Particularly since the introduction of the manmade fibers, blends have become so generally used that knowledge about them is of great importance to the consumer. Since the Textile Fiber Products Identification Act became effective in March 1960, the proportions (by weight) of the various fibers in a textile product must be made known on the label. Consumers, therefore, are told the amount of each fiber present. To use this information most effectively, the consumer must know the general characteristics of the various fibers, and their relative position with other fibers in these characteristics. He must also have some idea of the carry-over of fiber properties into blends and which criteria, such as amount of fiber present, determine the effectiveness of this carry-over. Fabric construction and finish also play a very important part in the characteristics of the final fabric. Therefore, the study of the characteristics of blends of fibers is usually undertaken on fabrics of similar construction and finish.

Elastomer Fiber Yarns

Elastic yarns are made from rubber, spandex, or anidex fibers. They differ from stretch yarns that are made by texturizing a thermoplastic filament because the recovery power of elastic yarns depends on the elastomer core, whereas in stretch yarns the recovery depends on the heat-setting of crimped filaments. The three basic kinds of elastic yarns are as follows:

Covered. A covered elastic yarn consists of a core of rubber, spandex, or anidex, wrapped singly or doubly with filament or staple yarns. Double-wrapped yarns are heavier and are used in a more durable fabric than the single-wrapped yarns. The covering allows for absorbency, improves the hand, and permits a color range. Covered elastic yarns are used for foundation garments, swim suits, suitings, and hosiery.

Core-spun. A core-spun elastic yarn is made by spinning a sheath of staple fiber around a core of spandex or anidex while the core is being stretched. Core-spun yarns give fabrics the appearance of being made with regular yarns. They are generally used to create a comfortable stretch-woven fabric for use as outerwear, for upholstery, or for slipcovers. Core-spun yarns are also used in knitted fabrics where more elasticity is desired.

Bare Elastic Yarn. A bare elastic yarn is simply the spandex or anidex elastomer monofilament yarn as it comes from the spinnerette. These yarns are less costly than other elastic yarns and are suitable for thin garments such as sheer foundation garments and sock tops. Bare elastic yarns or monofilaments, however, lack a pleasing hand such as that provided by the covering processes in other methods.

Metallic Yarns

Metallic yarns date back to Biblical times and were reserved for the apparel of the rich, the nobility, and the clergy. Gold and silver were hammered into extremely thin sheets, cut into narrow strips, then woven into fabrics. The result was spectacular but heavy, brittle, and expensive. Today gold and silver yarns are seldom used, but their effect has been duplicated by aluminum in combination with man-made substances. Modern metallic yarns are soft and light in weight and do not tarnish.

The most common process of manufacturing consists of coating a tissue-thin sheet of aluminum foil on either side with adhesive. A sheet of transparent plastic film (polyester, acetate, cellophane, or cellulose-acetate-butyrate) is applied to each side of the adhesive-coated foil. The assembly is then cut into narrow strips from ¼ to 1/120 of an inch for weaving with other yarns into fabrics.

The plastic film forms a protective coating and gives added strength. Of the films used, polyester is not only the strongest, but is also the least affected by heat and chemicals.

Color can be introduced in several ways: (1) in the adhesive that holds the "sandwich" construction together; (2) in a thermoplastic resin that is attached to either side of the foil and heated to fix the color; or (3) in the film on either side of the aluminum foil.

Fabrics that include metallic yarns can be laundered, but the method of laundering varies with the type of plastic film used. Hang tags and labels often give care instructions.

Plastic Yarns

In recent years experiments have been under way to create "yarns" of plastic by cutting sheets of plastic into thin strands which may be left flat or rolled into tubelike structure or double-folded. Plastic yarns are intended for use in making fabrics that are as easy to care for as plastic and at the same time are as pliable and porous as woven or knitted fabrics. Fabrics made from plastic yarns are intended chiefly for upholstery.

Thread

Thread for sewing, embroidery, and lace-making must be so constructed that it is adaptable to use in a hand or machine process and will be durable and satisfactory in the finished product.

A satisfactory sewing thread must have the following physical, chemical, and aesthetic characteristics as well as others demanded by the end-use of the item:

High strength and elasticity
Smooth surface
Dimensional stability
High friction resistance
Resistance to snarling
Good appearance or hand
Good sewability whether used for hand or machine sewing
Resistance to color loss
Resistance to degradation from sunlight, perspiration, and chemicals in finishes or laundry products

The fibers most commonly used in sewing threads are cotton, silk, linen, nylon, and polyester. Rubber, spandex, and anidex are used in elastic threads. The fiber determines basic characteristics that should relate to the fabric on which the thread is to be used and to the garment or other item to be made.

Types of Sewing Thread

Core-Spun Thread. This type of thread has a core made of one kind of fiber surrounded by a spun sheath of another. Core-spun stretch threads have a spandex or anidex core with a sheath of staple fibers. Core-spun regular sewing thread has a high strength fine filament polyester core around which is spun a sheath of high quality cotton fiber. The thread combines the good characteristics of polyester and cotton fibers.

Elastic Thread. Elastic threads are constructed of an elastic core covered with nylon or other fiber coating. They are used to obtain a gathered or shirred effect.

Monocord Sewing Thread. This type of thread is possible with the thermoplastic man-made fibers. Fibers or filaments for the thread are laid parallel and welded or bonded together into a thread with only one cord and no spin or twist. Monocord thread has a finer diameter, higher strength, and higher abrasion resistance than have the more familiar threads of conventional construction.

Multiplecord Plied Sewing Thread. Traditional sewing threads are of this type. They are made of single yarns, doubled and twisted in plied yarns, and then the several plied yarns are twisted together. For example, six-cord cotton consists of six single yarns first made into three two-ply yarns which are then twisted together. Spun polyester is made from staple polyester fibers twisted into yarns in a manner similar to mercerized cotton thread but is stronger than cotton and provides more "give" without breaking.

Bonded Multiplecord Thread. A plied or twisted thread may also be welded or bonded in manufacture to produce a bonded thread that does have some twist. It does not achieve all of the superior properties of the monocord thread. Nymo (Belding Corticelli) is an example of this type of thread.

Thread Numbering Systems

Cotton threads are usually sold by number with the smaller numbers indicating the coarser threads. For example:

No. 12 coarse
No. 50 medium
No. 100 fine

Size of silk sewing thread is indicated by a letter designation. For example, A is the fineness usually used for home sewing; D, a coarser thread, for buttonhole twist. The letter designation is also used with some nylon and polyester threads.

Fabric Construction

The term *fabric*, as used in this publication, can be defined as a "planar structure produced by interlaced yarns or fibers" [1] and felts made by interlocking fibers.

Basically, there are five methods by which fabrics are made. They are (1) weaving, (2) knitting, (3) interlocking of fibers including felting and fusing, (4) netting and lacemaking, and (5) braiding.

The Mali machine introduced late in 1965 may add a sixth method of making cloth, that of *stitch-bonding*. Warp yarns coming from a creel, and filling yarns laid in as a sheet, are bound together by a third system of yarns stitched in by means of chainstitchers.

Fabric construction contributes to the end-use of textile products through such aspects as appearance, hand, strength, dimensional stability, absorbency, warmth, transparency, and suitability for further decorative effects. In many fabric characteristics, weave plays a greater part than fiber or finish.

Weaving

Woven fabrics are made by the interlacing of two or more sets of yarns at right angles to produce a fabric. The lengthwise yarn is called warp (ends), the crosswise yarn, filling (picks).

The common types of weaves are the *plain* weave with variations to make a *rib* weave or a *basket* weave, the *twill* weave, the *satin* weave, the *leno* weave, the *Jacquard* weave, the simple figured or *dobby* weave, the *pile* weave, and the *double-cloth* weave. Plain, twill, and satin are usually considered the basic weaves.

Many interesting effects can be created by varying the standard weaves described in the following sections.

[1] *Standard Definitions of Terms Relating to Textile Materials*, D-123-68a, p. 25.

Plain Weave

The simplest of all weaves is the plain weave. Each filling yarn passes alternately over and under one warp yarn. Each warp yarn passes alternately over and under each filling yarn.

In making a crepe fabric, the principle of contraction is used. The non-lustrous crinkly surface hides the fact that a crepe fabric is a plain weave. The filling yarns may be of high twist and the warp yarns of low twist or vice versa. Another method is to give the warp yarns a **Z** twist and the filling yarns an **S** twist. Still another method is to vary the tension of both the warp and filling yarns on the loom.

Some examples of plain-weave fabrics are: crepe, taffeta, shantung, organdy, and muslin. The plain weave may also have variations which include the following:

Basket Weave. In this construction, two or more yarns are used in both the warp and filling direction. These groups of yarns are woven as one, producing a basket effect. Examples of basket-weave fabrics are: monk's cloth, hopsacking, basketweave coating fabrics.

Rib Weave. The filling yarns are larger in diameter than are the warp yarns. A rib weave produces a fabric in which fewer yarns per square inch are visible on the surface. Examples: broadcloth, poplin, faille, bengaline, grosgrain, ottoman.

Twill Weave

This weave is characterized by diagonal ridges formed by yarns which are exposed on the surface. These may vary in angle from a low slope to a very steep slope. Twill weaves are more closely woven, heavier, and sturdier than plain weaves of comparable fiber and yarn size. They can be produced in fancy designs. A common variation is the herringbone.

Satin Weave

The satin weave is characterized by floating yarns used to produce a high luster on one side of a fabric.

Warp yarns of low twist float or pass over four or more filling yarns. The low twist and the floating of the warp yarns, together with the fiber content, give a high degree of light reflection. High-twist yarns may be used for the filling. Weights of satin fabrics range from chiffon satin to heavy duchesse satin.

The *sateen* weave is similar to a satin construction except that in the sateen weave, the filling yarns float and are visible on the surface of the fabric. Examples: cotton sateen, damask (uses both satin and sateen weaves).

Leno or Gauze Weave

In the leno or gauze weave, warp yarns in pairs are crossed over each other in the form of a figure 8. Spacing between the yarns creates an open porous effect, and the crossing over keeps the yarns from slipping out of place readily. The leno weave is made with a doup attachment on a regular loom. The term, gauze weave, is sometimes applied to a plain woven low-count weave that is not leno. Example of leno weave: marquisette.

Figured Weaves

Complex (Jacquard Weave). Elaborate designs are woven by use of a special mechanism, known as the Jacquard head-motion, which is placed above a loom. Through this mechanism each warp yarn is individually controlled by rods which, in turn, are controlled by a series of punched cards. The perforations in the cards determine which warp yarns are raised as the filling yarn passes through to create the design. Examples: brocade, damask.

Simple (Dobby Weaves). Small figured or geometric designs, repeated throughout a fabric, are woven by use of a dobby attachment on a plain harness loom. This attachment may be regarded as a simplified Jacquard mechanism that controls the heddles of a loom. Examples: madras, birdseye, huck-a-back.

Pique (Cord) Weave. Pique weave, done with a dobby attachment, produces a fabric with ridges or wales held up by floats on the back.

In the better quality fabrics, stuffer yarns are laid under ridges to emphasize roundness. The wales usually run lengthwise except in birdseye and bullseye piques. Fabrics have a definite right and wrong side and tear more easily in the lengthwise direction. Examples: pique, bedford cord.

Double-Cloth Weave

This weave uses more than one set of warp or filling yarns. It may produce a cloth with two distinct faces or it may produce two distinct cloths held together by an extra yarn which may be cut if it is desired to separate the two cloths. Examples: separated double cloth, some pile fabrics; not separated, blanket cloth, some upholstery; two distinct faces, double damask.

Pile Weave

Pile weaving is the interlacing of sets of yarns in such a manner that one set forms loops or cut ends on the surface of the cloth. The background weave may be either a plain or a twill weave. Examples are velvet, velveteen, plush, corduroy, terry cloth, and frieze. (There are also knitted pile fabrics.)

To form the pile, five basic methods may be used to introduce the extra sets of yarn into the fabric. These differ as follows: (1) The pile is formed by a second warp or filling yarn which is suspended as a float or placed over a wire. (2) Another process uses a double-cloth method with five sets of yarns. ·(3) Still another uses the slack-tension method. (4) Pile is formed by use of the tufting method. (5) Chenille yarns are woven into the fabric to form the pile.

The depth of the pile is determined by the length of the float, the height of the wire, the space between the fabrics in double-cloth weaving, the amount of slack allowed or the length of the tuft yarn.

The durability of the pile depends on the way in which the yarn is inserted. In the V-type weave, the pile goes under only one warp yarn, and the extra set of yarns is cut each time it passes over the other yarn. In the W-type, the pile goes under and over two warp yarns and the extra set of yarns is cut every other time it passes over the perpendicular yarns. The W weave is the more durable. The pile is held in place by two crossing yarns.

In some fabrics like terry cloth and frieze the pile is not cut. It is also possible to have cut and uncut pile in the same fabric.

Slack Tension Method. This method uses two warp beams. Yarns coming from the warp pile beam are allowed to loosen or slacken between every third filling yarn insertion. The slackened warp yarns create loops which may be left as loops or sheared to produce a plush effect. Examples: terry cloth, shagbark gingham.

Tufting. A series of needles, each holding a yarn, is punched through from the underside of an already woven fabric. As the needles are withdrawn, they leave looped or cut yarns on the surface of the fabric. The yarns are then held in place through a process that (1) untwists the surface tuft or (2) coats the fabric with a backing compound or (3) shrinks the ground fabric. Examples: Bedspreads, carpets.

Knitting

Knitted fabrics are made by needles that form a series of interlocking loops from a single yarn or a set of yarns and connect these rows of loops or chains into a continuous piece of cloth. Knitted fabrics, like woven fabrics, can be made from any type of fiber or yarn and may vary in textures and degrees of transparency or opaqueness.

Commercial knitting started in the 16th century. Knitted fabrics are used most widely in underwear, hosiery, and sweaters and other sportswear, where the stretch and wrinkle-resistance which result from the knitting process are highly desirable.

The air pockets created by knitting serve as insulators and add to both the warmth and the absorbency of knitted fabrics. The pattern of stitches can be varied to produce decorative surface effects. Variety can also be achieved by combining, dropping, and adding stitches.

Quality and serviceability of knitted fabrics will depend on the type of knitting used, the fiber, the fineness and evenness of the yarn, closeness of the knitting, and the dimensional stability of the finished fabric, as well as dyes and special finishes.

In women's hosiery, *denier* indicates the fineness of the yarn used. *Gauge* indicates the number of stitches per inch-and-one-half on the needle bar.

There are two basic types of knitting machines: (1) flat needle bar type that produces a flat fabric similar to a loom product and (2) circular type that produces a circular tube of fabric.

Knits are basically classified according to the method of knitting: weft or warp.

Weft Knitting

This is a circular or flat knitting process that places one yarn at a time to form loops running across the fabric. Weft knitting may be done by hand or by a jersey, a purl, or a rib knit machine. Weft knits can be classified according to the machine or to the stitch such as plain, jersey, purl, and rib with interlock or Jacquard variations. The process can produce either finished garments or lengths of fabric for clothing or upholstery. Examples: jersey, hosiery, furlike fabrics, sweaters, double-knits.

Warp Knitting

This is a flat knitting process with one or more sets of yarns that run vertically and parallel to each other. The warp yarns are interlocked to form vertical wales on the face of the fabric. The basic types of warp knitting machines are:

Milanese. This machine produces a fabric with two sets of yarns that are knitted opposite to each other in a diagonal formation. The face of the fabric has a very fine rib with a diagonal structure on the back. The fabric is runproof; intended chiefly for gloves and lingerie.

Raschel. Multiple bars and latch needles provide a great variety of fabrics—in plain or Jacquard patterns, in lacy or dense textures, in stable or elastic forms. Examples: lace, power net, men's suiting, blankets.

Simplex. This machine has two needle and guide bars and is similar to the tricot machine. Simplex knits are double-faced fabrics, used primarily for gloves and swimwear.

Tricot. Generically "tricot" refers to all warp-knit fabrics. Specifically it applies to fabric with the plain jersey stitch produced on the tricot machine. The fabric may be called jersey, tricot, or tricot jersey and may be further distinguished as one-, two-, or three-bar tricot according to the kinds of guide bars that control the fabric in the making. The machine can be modified to create tuck stitch, Jacquard, and other designs. Examples: jersey, matte jersey.

Double Knitting

A type of knitting using two sets of needles. Fabrics have more body and durability than single knits and are less likely to sag or lose shape.

Interlocking of Fibers

These processes produce felts and nonwoven fabrics.

Felting

Felting is the oldest method of fabric construction. It depends on the property of wool fibers to coil and mat together and to so entangle themselves that they become permanently interlocked. Because of this property, the fibers can be made to form a dense, strong material. In the manufacture of felt, fibers are compressed together by the application of heat, moisture, agitation, and pressure. The resulting fabric is fulled to strengthen and shrink it to the desired thickness and firmness. Chemical action may also be used in making felt. True felt contains all-wool or part-wool fibers. Finishing processes may include dyeing and any of several special finishes to make the felt mothproof, mildew-resistant, flame-resistant, or resistant to soil and water.

Both the fiber used and the construction of felt contribute to its excellent resilience and abrasion resistance. In industry, felt has an infinite number of uses where its combination of resilience and hardness is important.

For consumer uses, felt serves as an insulating and sound-deadening material and is used for decorative purposes and in apparel. It is warm, resilient, and has the capacity to "breathe," though compared to woven or knitted fabrics, its tensile strength is low.

Felt is non-fraying and its edges do not need finishing. Weight, strength, color, and finishes can be chosen for the end-use desired.

Nonwoven Fabrics

Glazed wadding, the forerunner of today's nonwoven fabrics, was made as early as 1860. Today millions of pounds of fiber are consumed annually by the nonwoven fabric industry. The techniques and processes are covered by numerous patents.

Nonwoven fabrics can be made with a wide range of properties. They have two major textile end-uses: disposable textile products, and interior elements of garments or other items where they are used for padding, shaping, or reinforcement. Specific applications include filters for air and liquids, heat and electrical insulation, packaging, bandages and other medical products, backing for plastics and leathers, fillers for quilted structures, toweling, wall covering, curtains and draperies, coated fabrics, book bindings, luggage, and ribbons.

Nonwovens are currently made by fusing a bonded web or by fusing continuous filaments as they are randomly extruded from the spinnerette or by needle punching.

Fusing A Bonded Web. Four steps are involved in this process: (1) Opening and blending fibers, (2) forming a web, (3) applying binder, (4) drying and curing.

Fibers in a web can be oriented or laid at random and bonded by one of four methods: (1) saturation of the complete web or mat with adhesive, (2) spraying of the carded webs or mats with an adhesive or solvent and drying without pressure, (3) discontinuous bonding applied in strips or printed so that most of the fabric is not bonded, (4) fusion and pressure.

Binders may be solution binders such as starch and polyvinyl alcohol, polymer emulsions, thermoplastic fibers intermixed in the web, or synthetic polymers deposited in powdered form and heated.

Fusing Continuous Filaments. By this process, filaments extruded from the spinnerette are electrostatically deposited, in random fashion, on a fast moving belt and then fused together by heat and pressure. The result is a very strong, washable fabric for clothing and carpet backing.

Needle Punching. In this process a prepared web of fibers is passed over a board with barbed needles which are thrust up and down through the web, causing the fibers to interlock mechanically into a firm, compact mass. Examples: patio carpeting, blankets.

The properties of nonwoven fabrics can be built in to match end-use requirements. In purchasing nonwoven fabrics, the consumer may select from fabrics varying in strength, bulk, weight, relative stiffness or softness, and flexibility. He should consider dimensional stability, colorfastness, absorbency, hand, linting, and appearance where these properties are important to the end-use.

Netting and Lacemaking

Lacemaking became a fine art in Italy over the period of time from 1300 to 1500. The bobbinet machine which became the basis for today's lace machines was patented in 1808. Lace was first made by machine in 1813. Several of the most common types of machine-made laces sold today are:

Leavers method: Alençon, Chantilly, Cluny, filet, malines, Milan, tulle, Valenciennes

Bobbinet method: commercial nets, filet, malines, net appliqué, point d'esprit, tulle

Nottingham method: filet, net, Nottingham

Schiffli method: Breton, Cluny, Point de Venise, Richelieu

Of course, there are still many types of handmade laces. Only study and handling of laces will help one learn to tell them apart.

Laces may be used either as fabrics for entire garments or household items, or as decorative or trimming elements.

The use of the man-made fibers in lace has enlarged the variety of laces available at moderate cost and has greatly simplified the problem of caring for lace. The range of price and the quality of lace vary greatly and depend upon such factors as the fiber used, the intricacy of the design, whether the lace is machine- or handmade, domestic or imported.

Braiding

In braiding, three or more yarns are interlaced lengthwise and diagonally to form a fabric. An early example of braiding was the handmade braided rug Today, complex braids are made for trim or for unusual garments.

Stitch Bonding

Stitch bonding or knit-sew is a compartively new method of making a fabric commercially from a mat of yarns systematically arranged. A threaded needle passes through the basic structure of yarns causing inter-connected loops or a chainstitch to be formed. Rows of this stitching hold the structure as a solid fabric. For this process Malimor, Arachne, and Krotomatic machines are used. Production in the United States is limited. In Europe, unusual drapery and decorative fabrics have been produced at a very economical rate. Diapers, underwear, carpets, and blankets are also made on these machines.

Bonded and Laminated Fabrics

The 1968 Book of ASTM Standards, Part 24, p. 612, differentiates between bonded and laminated fabrics as follows:

Bonded fabric: a layered fabric structure wherein a face or shell fabric is joined to a backing fabric such as tricot, with an adhesive that does not significantly add to the thickness of the combined fabrics.

Laminated fabric: a layered fabric structure wherein a face or outer fabric is joined to a continuous sheet material such as polyurethane foam either by the flame-bonding method or by an adhesive, and this, in turn, is usually though not always joined with a backing fabric such as tricot.

Bonded fabrics have many desirable qualities. They have a built-in lining which may provide skin-side comfort. They have good stretch and recovery and may give garments a stable structure. Laminated fabrics are wrinkle-resistant, have good tailoring possibilities, and provide insulation with low weight.

Recently a number of organizations have established standards to cope with such problems as shrinking, delamination, puckering, and blistering of bonded fabrics. But whether the standards will eliminate or merely alleviate these problems remains to be seen.

Stretch Fabrics

Stretch properties can be imparted to fabrics by the type of fiber, yarn, or fabric construction used. A slack mercerization finish can impart stretch to an all-cotton fabric.

Stretch means the property of textile fibers, yarns, and fabrics which (1) enables them, or materials made from them, to be extended substantially in either width or length or both under forces customarily encountered in textile use application and (2) causes the materials to contract to practically their original dimensions upon removal of the forces, either instantaneously or within a brief period of time.

There are two kinds of stretch—power stretch and comfort stretch. Power stretch is important in garments and other items that require holding power and elasticity. Power stretch garments support muscles and body organs, reduce body size, and firm and shape body flesh. Comfort stretch, as the name implies, provides elasticity for the comfort of the wearer. Comfort stretch fabrics may not look any different from non-stretch fabrics.

Power Stretch. The use of elastic fibers (rubber, spandex, and anidex) in a fabric can produce power stretch properties. Rubber must be covered, but anidex and spandex can be used bare or as a very fine core of a spun yarn. Fabrics made of elastic fibers are excellent for swimwear and foundation garments.

Comfort Stretch. Thermoplastic fibers can be twisted and heat-set to produce texturized stretch yarns. Fabrics woven from these yarns and from core-spun yarns have comfort stretch. Fabrics knitted from stretch yarns can be used for very close-fitting garments such as hosiery and leotards.

Cotton Stretch Fabrics. Stretch properties are imparted to cotton yarns and fabrics by three main methods: (1) Insertion of stretch characteristics into all-cotton yarn by means of twisting-untwisting methods similar to those used for the stretch yarns of man-made fibers. This requires a combination of (a) application of chemicals which facilitate the cross-linking of the molecules in the cotton fiber to make them resilient and (b) mechanical processes which can twist, heat-set, and untwist in a single process at speeds that are economically sound.

(2) Fabric finishing techniques such as slack mercerization. Fabrics given stretch by this method may also acquire improved hand, drape, and luster, and show less seam puckering.

(3) Combination of fabric construction with lively or torque yarns. In this process, the torque is put into the yarn and a suitable type of fabric production is chosen.

Stretch cotton fabrics may be given a 25 to 30 percent stretch, but an 8 to 15 percent stretch

is considered a good "working" stretch. Stretch may be applied in the filling or warp or both.

Stretch cotton fabrics are being used in foundation garments, diapers, sportswear, uniforms, gloves, slipcovers to simplify selection and care of the items or improve wearing comfort.

Shrinkage of Fabrics

Shrinkage may occur in a fiber because of its physical or chemical properties. When the fibers are made into yarns and these yarns are woven into fabrics, the factors that affect shrinkage become very complicated.

Felting Shrinkage. Felting shrinkage may occur in fabrics made of wool and hair fibers. These fibers have a natural tendency to felt—that is, to shorten and mat together—because of their scaly surface. This is called felting shrinkage. The tendency to mat is very pronounced in Angora and other rabbit fibers, more so than in wool or other hair fibers. Woolen fabrics containing even small percentages of Angora tend to shrink more readily than do all-wool fabrics. Soft, loosely woven wool fabrics, especially those of high-grade wool fibers, have a tendency to felt more than do hard-finished wool fabrics.

Felting shrinkage can result from: (1) excessive mechanical action during laundering or drycleaning and drying, (2) high temperature along with tumbling action in drying, and (3) high relative humidity of the solvent during drycleaning.

Mechanical action, moisture, and heat—the very forces that are employed to produce felt—must be applied with caution in handling fabrics where felting is not desired. Once a fabric has become felted, it is impossible to stretch it back to its original size.

Chemical finishes employing chlorine or bromine gas or melamine formaldehyde resin on wool fabrics are used to help control shrinkage.

Progressive Shrinkage. Both relaxation shrinkage and swelling shrinkage seldom reach their maximum in the first cleaning (laundering or drycleaning). These forms of shrinkage continue through successive cleanings. This is called progressive shrinkage.

Progressive shrinkage may not become noticeable until the third or fourth cleaning in an overstretched, sized fabric. Maximum shrinkage has been reached in tests from the second to tenth cleaning.

Relaxation Shrinkage. Most fabrics are produced under tension. These tensions leave strains in the fabric. Unless these strains are fully released by the manufacturer before the fabric is made into a garment, relaxation shrinkage will ultimately occur. Relaxation shrinkage is the tendency of the yarns to revert to their normal, unstretched dimensions. In many cases, sizings or finishes help keep the fabric in its stretched condition.

If a fabric has not been fully relaxed by the manufacturer, drycleaning or laundering will cause the fabric to continue its relaxation and shrinkage. Usually several cleanings will be required to relax it completely. Laundering or drycleaning may partially or wholly remove any sizings or finishes which tend to stabilize the fabric dimensions.

Shrinkage of Bias-Cut Garments. Bi-symmetrical circular-cut skirts may shrink (1) in the center front and center back, or (2) at each of the side seams, depending on (a) the construction of the fabric, and (b) the relative direction of the warp yarns and the filling yarns to the cut of the garment. The majority of fabrics shrink to the greatest degree in the warp or lengthwise direction. Therefore if a skirt is cut with the filling yarns of the fabric at the center front and center back, shrinkage is most likely to occur at each side seam. If the warp yarns are parallel to the center front and center back and side seams parallel to the filling yarns, the skirt may shrink at the center front and center back.

Bias-cut garments may shrink in drycleaning, wetcleaning, laundering, or steam-pressing. Preshrinkage of fabrics before garment construction is therefore recommended.

Shrinkage in Fabric Combinations. In some cases, two different fabrics that have very different shrinkage characteristics may be combined in a garment or household item. For example, a drapery or dress fabric may shrink more than its lining. The reverse might also be true. Only fabric combinations which do not differ in their shrinkage characteristics should be combined in garment design.

Shrinkage in Pressing or Finishing. Some fibers and some fabric constructions—particularly wool and thermoplastics—are softened when steamed and pressed. As a result, they relax and shrink during pressing. This type of shrinkage may occur in drycleaning or laundering when items are finished on steam- and air-finishing equipment.

Some wool fabrics sold as piece goods are not preshrunk during textile manufacture. It is a good practice to have these fabrics steamed to relax them before they are made up into garments. Fabrics made of the heat-sensitive fibers should bear identifying labels as a guide to proper handling in cleansing.

Swelling Shrinkage. When fibers pick up moisture, they swell. This can cause shrinkage in rib-weave fabrics and in rib variations, such as some failles, gros de Londres, épinglés, grosgrains, bengalines, ottomans, and in fabrics of other constructions. Shrinkage is usually greatest in the rib-weave fabrics made of wool, rayon, cotton, acetate, or a combination of any of these. For example, a rayon or acetate yarn may be used in the warp or lengthwise direction of a fabric that has a heavy crosswise rib of rayon or cotton. These rib fibers swell more than do the acetate warps when wet. When they swell, they pull the ribs close together, and shrinkage occurs. Rayon used in the warp may shrink also.

Rib-weave or other fabrics susceptible to swelling shrinkage may be preshrunk in the finishing plant, though the relaxation of rib-weave fabrics is more difficult than that of others. Rib-weave fabrics, not known to be preshrunk, should be cleaned in a drycleaning solvent with low relative humidity. Wetcleaning or laundering may cause excessive shrinkage.

Finishes

Finishes include all the processes that follow the construction of a fabric until it is ready for use. They contribute so much to the final character and appearance of the fabric that it is often said that it is the finish that makes the fabric. Finishes provide the added qualities desired for a particular fabric and may be used to counteract an undesirable quality of a particular fiber or fabric. Many finishes give more than one property to a fabric.

Not all finishes have names used as promotional devices. The label, however, may indicate which finishes have been applied to the fabric. Other finishes do have trademark names that appear on labels or hang tags and are used in advertising to the consumer. Some examples of trademark names are included in this chapter.

In the following sections, finishes are defined and classified according to reasons for their use.

To Improve Appearance and Texture

Bleaching. The whitening of textiles and removal of impurities in fabrics by the use of chemicals such as peroxide or chlorine bleaching compounds.

Calendering. A finishing process of pressing fabric between rollers to make it smooth and glossy. Various conditions of heat, pressure, and tension will produce different effects. May be used with chemical treatment to obtain special surfaces.

Carbonizing. The chemical removal of vegetable matter from wool. When wool is dry the carbonized matter "dusts off" in a mechanical crushing operation. A process also used on reused wool.

Crabbing. A wool finishing process to prevent creases or other forms of uneven shrinkage in later stages of finishing. The fabric is treated with boiling water to set or fix the yarns permanently.

Decating or **Decatizing.** A finishing process applied to fabrics to set the material, enhance luster, and improve the hand. The cloth is wound around a perforated drum, between layers of a blanket, and steam passed through from the inside to outside layers. The action is then reversed and steam removed by vacuum pump on completion of treatment. This process may help overcome uneven or blotchy dyeing.

Degumming. A scouring operation which removes the natural gum from silk in a hot soap solution. Degumming is usually performed after the yarn has been woven or knitted.

Fulling. A finishing process in the woolen industry which involves the application of moisture, heat, friction, and pressure. It results in felting of the wool and may produce varied effects depending upon the extent of the process.

Scouring. The removal of dirt, natural waxes, processing oils, and sizing, which accumulated on yarns during weaving, by washing with soap or synthetic detergent.

Tentering. The mechanical straightening and drying of fabrics. If the fabric is not dried so that the filling yarns are exactly perpendicular to the warp yarns, it will be off grain. After resin finishes have been applied, or after thermoplastic fibers have been heat-set, an off grain cannot be corrected.

To Roughen and Dull

Delustering. The natural sheen of man-made yarns and fabrics may be reduced or eliminated during finishing by use of various chemicals or special heat treatments. Any desired luster in fibers may be produced by inclusion of a finely divided pigment in the spinning solution. The cross-section of the spinnerette openings may also affect the luster.

Flocking. The attachment of very short fibers to the surface of a fabric by use of an adhesive. Some fabrics resemble suede or velour.

Napping and Gigging. The use of fine metal hooks or teasels on cylinders to pull fiber ends to the surface and produce the nap.

To Make Smooth and Lustrous

Beetling. A process in which linen or cotton cloth, wrapped on a wooden core, is pounded to give a flat effect. Instead of wood, an iron core may be used to produce a moiré effect. The result is a soft, full, thready finish which gives cotton goods the appearance of linen.

Brushing. The removal of short, loose fibers from the surface of the fabric by mechanical means.

Ciré Finishing. The production of a high polish by use of wax or a thermoplastic substance and a friction calendar. This type of finish gives fabrics the "wet" look.

Glazing. The production of a shiny, slick surface by use of a friction calender and various chemicals. Nondurable finishes involve starch, glue, etc., whereas durable finishes are resins. Prolonged life of these finishes requires care in the laundering and drycleaning of the fabric.

Mercerization. Mercerization—primarily applied to cotton fabrics—is the treatment of cotton with 18 to 20 percent sodium hydroxide. If the mercerization is done while the fabric is held under tension, the result is a stronger, more lustrous fabric with increased ability to accept dyes. If the fabric is mercerized without tension (slack mercerization), the fibers and yarns within the fabric swell and contract. This increases the amount of crimp in the yarns which, in turn, allows the fabric, when pulled, to stretch more than an untreated fabric. Most of the 100 percent cotton stretch fabrics currently available are made by this process. The recovery from stretching of slack mercerized fabrics can be improved by further treatment with a wrinkle-resistant finish.

Schreinering. The use of a calender containing as many as 250 lines per inch engraved on the diagonal. This finish is used frequently on cotton fabrics for soft luster or on nylon and polyester tricot to flatten the yarns and give an opaque appearance.

Singeing. The burning off of projecting fibers and yarn ends to obtain a smooth surface. Thermoplastic fibers melt.

To Change Weight, Flexibility, and Hand

Weighting. The addition of metallic salts or gums to add weight to silk fabrics.

Sizing. A general term for compounds which, when added to yarn or fabric, form a more or less continuous solid film around the yarn and individual fibers. Sizing may be applied to increase strength, smoothness, stiffness, or weight. Sizing agents may be temporary (e.g., starch) or durable (e.g., thermosetting and thermoplastic resins).

Parchmentizing. The production of transparent, permanently stiff cotton fabrics (e.g., organdy) by treatment with sulfuric acid.

Crisp Finish. Chemical finishes applied to cotton, rayon, or nylon sheers to make them stay crisp during wear, laundering, wetcleaning, and drycleaning. Such finishes will also help to keep corners of sheer fabrics from rolling. *Fresh-Tex* (Cranston) is one such finish.

Softening. The use of various agents to improve the hand and drape of a fabric. Softeners seal down fiber ends and lubricate fibers and yarns so that they move readily; softeners may increase the life of fabrics. These agents include: oil, fat, and wax emulsions; silicone compounds; and substituted ammonium compounds.

To Increase Serviceability

Antiseptic Finish (Anti-Bacterial or Bacteriostatic). A chemical treatment designed to make a fabric bacteria-resistant, and to prevent decay and damage from perspiration. The treatment inhibits the growth of a broad spectrum of bacteria, including odor-causing germs. The chemicals used include quaternary ammonium compounds and metallic salts or organic compounds. Some antiseptics are also claimed to be mildew-resistant. A trademark name is *Sanitized* (Sanitized, Inc.).

Anti-Static Finish. A chemical treatment applied to a fabric to prevent the accumulation of static electricity. Static electricity generated in a fabric makes it cling to the wearer or to other garments. It also has the power to attract and hold soil. The hydrophobic man-made fibers tend to accumulate static electricity. Hydrophilic fibers, such as cotton and rayon, usually contain sufficient water to dissipate electrical charges before static electricity is formed.

An anti-static finish adds a water-attracting chemical to the fabric and thus endows the hydrophobic fabric with the ability to attract and retain water which will carry off the electric charges.

There are many anti-static finishes used by textile finishing companies. They may be applied to loose, yarn, or piece form to prevent electrostatic charges being built up during processing or in subsequent wear. A product for home use is *Negastat* (Playtime Products, Inc.) an anti-static solution added to final rinse water.

Crush-Resistant Finish. A resin treatment applied to pile fabrics to enable them to recover from crushing.

Flame-Retardant Finish. Fabrics or articles that usually are flammable are treated in such a way as to render them incapable of supporting combustion when the original source of the flame is no longer in contact with the treated material. However, treatment does not produce a fireproof fabric. (See Flammable Fabrics Act, page —.) Since the passage of the 1967 Amendments to the Act, many different products are required to meet federal flammability standards. However, much more remains to be done.

Flame-retardant finishes act in different ways including (1) catalyzing the dehydration reaction during the pyrolysis of cellulose which results in the formation of larger carbonaceous aggregates that do not oxidize as readily as smaller volatile decomposition products and thus inhibit flaming; (2) releasing substances to hasten cellulose degradation and the release of volatile products to inhibit flaming; (3) releasing gases or foams that smother flame.

Flame-retardant finishes may be temporary or relatively durable. The latter are complex organic materials that contain elements such as phosphorus, nitrogen, bromine, chlorine, or antimony. An important example of such a finish is tetrakis hydroxymethyl phosphonium chloride (THPC). Some trademark names for flame-retardant finishes are:

Flameproof 462-5 (Apex Chemical)
Firestop (Ameritex)
Pyroset (American Cyanamid)
Cav-Guard FR (Cavedon Chemical)
Pyrovatex CP (Ciba-Geigy Corporation)
Fire-Guard (Polymer Research)

It is important that type of finish be appropriate to fiber content, construction, and anticipated end-use of the fabric. Care in use and maintenance is required for retention of the fire-retardant property.

Flame-retardant solutions that can be applied by home methods to household fabrics [1] are:

Solution A (do not use on rayon or resin-treated cotton)
Borax, 7 ounces
Boric acid, 3 ounces
Hot water, 2 quarts
Solution B
Borax, 6 ounces
Diammonium phosphate, 6 ounces
Water, 2 quarts
Solution C (for rayon or resin-treated cotton fabrics)
Diammonium phosphate, 12 ounces
Water, 2 quarts
Solution D
Ammonium sulfate, 13 ounces
Water, 2 quarts
Household ammonia, small amount

Fume-Fading Resistant Finish. A finish used on acetate and *Arnel* (triacetate) fabrics to prevent color changes caused by oxides of nitrogen in the atmosphere. The fading is counteracted by change in the physical surface properties of the acetate fiber. Some of these finishes are fairly durable; others may be removed when the garment is laundered or drycleaned.

Mildew-Resistant Finish. A chemical finish applied to a fabric to prevent growth of mildew and mold. It is used on fabrics such as rayon, cotton, and linen, which, when untreated, are subject to attack by mildew in moist, humid

---

[1] From *Making Household Fabrics Flame Resistant*, Leaflet No. 454, U.S. Department of Agriculture, December 1959 (Revised 1967). For sale by the Superintendent of Documents, Government Printing Office, Washington, D. C. 20401. Price 5 cents.

conditions or climates. This finish may be combined with other finishes, such as water-repellents. *Fresh-Tex* (Cranston) includes mildew-resistance as a quality it imparts to fabrics.

Moth-Resistant Finish. A chemical treatment of wool to make it resistant to attack by moths and carpet beetles. Various processes differ in their resistance to laundering and drycleaning, and in the length of time they are effective.

Fabrics may be treated with moth-resistant or mothproofing finishes of various kinds.

Some trademark names are:

Mitin (Ciba-Geigy Corporation)

Moth Snub (Arkansas Company)

Woolgard (Apex Chemical Company)

Perspiration-Resistant Finish. A chemical finish applied to a fabric to make it resistant to the damage caused by body perspiration. Such damage may include loss of color and loss of strength. This finish finds widest application in fabrics used for garment linings.

Some trademark names are:

Sanitized (Sanitized, Inc.)

Unifast and *Unidye* (United Piece Dye Works) impart other properties as well as perspiration resistance.

Shrink-Resistant Finish. Shrinkage of fabrics may be controlled by either chemical or mechanical methods.

Chemical Methods. Wrinkle-resistant treatments with resins very often provide shrinkage control for fabrics made from cellulosic fibers. Resin impregnation of fibers can result in stabilizing a fabric, thus controlling shrinkage or stretching of the fabric in laundering or drycleaning.

Chemical methods are also used for controlling the felting shrinkage of wool. The two types of treatment most often used for this purpose are (1) controlled oxidation of the wool—often by chlorination, and (2) interfacial polymerization which deposits a very thin resin coating over the surface of the wool fiber. A commonly used trade name for the first type of treatment is *Dylanized* (Stevens Dyers, Ltd.). The second type of treatment was developed at the western regional laboratory of the U. S. Department of Agriculture and named *Wurlan*. Several commercial finishes of this type have been developed, e.g.,

Bancora (Joseph Bancroft) and *Zeset* (du Pont) are such products.

A combination of chlorination and resin coating is found in the *Hercosett* (Hercules, Inc.) and *Superwash* (Wool Bureau) processes.

Mechanical Methods. In the textile mill, relaxation shrinkage is eliminated by overfeeding a fabric onto a drying frame and applying stretch in the crosswise direction of the fabric. It may also be eliminated by applying controlled compression forces parallel to the surface of the fabric, pushing together the warp yarns, thus releasing the weaving strains. Fabrics so treated may have less than 2 percent shrinkage in the warp and filling direction.

The trademark *Sanforized* (Sanforized Co.) applied to cotton or linen fabrics indicates a mechanical shrink-resistant finish that has met standards of less than 1 percent shrinkage when the fabric is air- (not tumble-) dried.

Heat-setting is used on fabrics or articles made from thermoplastic fibers to give dimensional stability, improve resiliency and elastic recovery, and produce relatively permanent design details (pleats, planned creases, or surface embossing). The fabric or article is held in the desired shape and size, an amount of heat (which depends upon the type of fiber) is applied to cause softening, and the product is allowed to cool in the desired position. During maintenance of heat-set articles, laundering, drying, and ironing temperatures must be kept below the heat-setting temperature.

Slip-Resistant Finish. This finish is applied to a fabric to keep yarns in place so that they will not slip over one another. It also serves to keep seams from fraying. The finish has received wide application in fabrics made of the man-made fibers.

Soil Release Finish. With the advent of durable press fabrics, the removal of certain types of soil has become a problem. Oil type stains, often found on men's shirt collars, or grease stains, especially on work trousers, are more difficult to remove from durable press fabrics than from untreated cottons. To help solve this problem, a number of finishes have been developed for use on durable press fabrics. These have been called *soil release* or *SR* finishes. Many durable press fabrics have had this type of finish applied, but the results to date have not been 100 percent effective. Better SR finishes will have to be developed and used satisfactorily before the problem of oil type stains on durable press fabrics can be considered solved.

Chemicals used in soil release include hydrophilic copolymers, acrylate emulsions, and fluorocarbons. They act either to form a hydrophilic surface that attracts water and allows it to lift off the soil, or they coat the fibers so soil cannot penetrate. They may also act as anti-static agents, prevent soil redeposition, and improve fabric hand. Some trademark names are:

Cirrasol-PT (ICI America, Inc.)
Dual-action Scotchgard (Minnesota Mining and Manufacturing Co.)
Fantessa (J. P. Stevens & Co.)
Multi-action Zepel (du Pont)
Visa (Deering Milliken, Inc.)
Zelcon (du Pont)

Stain- and Spot-Resistant Finish. These finishes help to protect fabrics from spills. Some are water repellents which resist waterborne stains only. Others resist both oil- and waterborne stains. Many of these are durable to washing and drycleaning. However, thorough rinsing after cleaning is essential since any detergent which remains on the fabric will mask the finish and interfere with stain resistance. Laundering and abrasion during wear tend to reduce the stain resistance, especially the resistance to oil-borne stains of the water- and oil-repellent finishes. Pressing after laundering helps to restore stain resistance. Laundering may not always remove oil-borne stains from some stain-resistant fabrics, and it may be necessary to spot clean them with solvent.

Zepel (du Pont) and *Scotchgard* (Minnesota Mining and Manufacturing) are trade names for two durable fluorochemical finishes which resist water- and oil-borne stains. *Hydro-Pruf* (Arkansas) and *Syl-Mer* (Dow Chemical) are trade names for two durable silicone finishes which resist waterborne stains.

Thermal-Insulative Finish. An applied coating which can increase warmth or coolness, depending upon the situation. Aluminum coatings are used for drapery and garment linings. For the latter, however, such coatings have proved to be ineffective. In hot weather the metallic coating on draperies reflects solar heat and in winter retains heat. Some metallic finishes dryclean very well; others lose part or all of the metallic particles in drycleaning. Performance depends upon the base fabric, the binder used, and the conditions of the curing time. *Milium* (Deering Milliken) is an example of a metal-insulated lining fabric.

Waterproof Finish. This finish is made by applying rubber, lacquer, linseed oil compounds, or a synthetic resin to the fabric. These materials close the pores of the fabric and enable it to shed water under all pressures. These fabrics do not breathe. Some of these materials stiffen in drycleaning. Fabrics so treated should be wet-cleaned.

Microporous finishes or coating for apparel fabrics are said to waterproof the fabric for all weather conditions while still allowing it to "breathe." To make microporous material, a resin or synthetic rubber compound is mixed with a pore-forming material and applied to the fabric. During a subsequent heating process, the inserted material swells, producing a cell structure of interconnected, microscopically small particles. In a special bath, the material is then leached out of the fabric, leaving the microscopic pores. *Reevair* (Reeves Brothers) is one trademark name for microporous coated fabrics.

Water-Repellent Finish. This finish makes a fabric resistant to wetting but not waterproof. A water-repellent finish permits a fabric to breathe, allowing passage of air, water vapor, and perspiration. Water-repellent fabrics are more comfortable to wear than are waterproofed fabrics. Some finishes are called "durable"; others are "non-durable" to drycleaning. These latter may be labeled "renewable," meaning that they can be renewed by the drycleaner. Some trademark names are:

Cravenette (Cravenette Company)
Zelan (du Pont)

Wool Presensitizing. This process (WB-5, developed by the Wool Bureau) presensitizes all-wool fabrics for permanent pleating and creasing. Dyed wool fabrics are presensitized at the mill with a special, non-resinous, wool-setting chemical (monoethanolamine sulfite), which, once applied, remains in the wool fabric until it is activated with water and steam. When so activated, it sets the formed pleats or creases permanently. Fabrics so treated will still be subject to the normal felting shrinkage when agitated in water and detergent; therefore, the permanently pleated or creased garments should be drycleaned rather than laundered.

Wrinkle-Resistant Finishes (Wash-and-Wear Finish; Durable or Permanent Press). Because the cellulosic fibers have very poor elastic recovery and resilience, they wrinkle easily and fail to recover fully from wrinkling after a stress is removed. For this reason the wrinkle-resistant finishes have been developed for application on cotton, linen, and rayon fabrics as well as fabrics made from blends or combinations of these fibers with others such as nylon, acrylic, polyester, or triacetate. These finishes improve both the shape retention and the wrinkle recovery of the treated fabric. According to the most accepted theory, the finishes crosslink the cellulose molecules and in that way improve the elastic properties.

Several types of finishes which will improve resilience have been developed. These include both nitrogen-containing cross-linking agents (the most-used type) and non-nitrogenous cross-linking agents. Proper selection from among these finishes or combinations of these plus proper selection of the finishing conditions can produce fabrics having a wide variety of properties such as: (1) high dry-wrinkle resistance and muss resistance; high wrinkle recovery in the dry state plus good wrinkle recovery when wet; (2) excellent wrinkle recovery when wet plus moderate wrinkle resistance and recovery when dry; (3) excellent wrinkle recovery and wrinkle resistance in both the wet and dry states combined with the possibility of durable creases, pleats, and seams in finished garments.

The precure process involves applying the chemicals to the fabric and curing with heat to effect cross-linking and resin formation. The fabric is then shipped to the garment manufacturer. In the postcure process the fabric finish is applied at the mill and dried (or, perhaps, partially cured) before the fabric goes to the garment manufacturer. After the garment has been cut, sewn, and pressed, final curing of the fabric finish is obtained by means of either oven baking or pressing with high temperatures and pressures. This is known as the postcure process.

A possible limitation to this type of finish is the difficulty in altering durably-pressed garments. In addition, the harsh curing conditions currently used cause excessive damage to the abrasion resistance of the cellulosic components. Consequently, many durably-pressed garments are produced from fabrics containing a substantial amount (25 to 65 percent) of nylon or polyester fiber blended with the cotton.

Additional advantages that may be gained from the use of wrinkle-resistant finishes are: (1) durable crispness and body so that no starching is needed; (2) control of relaxation shrinkage; and (3) the production of durable surface effects by combining resin treatment and calendering of the fabric.

Problems that have been encountered with the finishes are: (1) chlorine retention by the nitrogen-containing resins (but not by the other two types of finish); (2) off-grain finish that could not be straightened; (3) reduced strength, tear strength, and abrasion resistance of the fabric; and (4) greater retention of oil-borne stains. Because of the latter problem, these fabrics are sometimes given a soil release finish. Users should read labels on any wrinkle-resistant garment to see whether or not a chlorine-containing bleach may be used. Hydrogen peroxide and other peroxygen type bleaches may be used on fabrics containing these finishes, providing any dyes present are stable to the bleaches.

The wash-and-wear finish or process itself may have a trademark name such as *Sanforized-Plus* (Sanforized Company) or may be indicated by a fabric name such as:

Belfast (non-resin type) (Deering Milliken)
Everglaze, BanCare, Minicare (Joseph Bancroft)
Super-Kwik-Kare (Reeves Brothers)
Perma-Pressed (Avondale Mills)
Tebilized (T. B. Lee). Wrinkle-resistance for linens, cottons, spun rayon.
Wrinkl-Shed (Dan River Mills). Permanent wrinkle-resistant finish for cotton fabrics.

Some durable press trademark names are:
Koratron (Koret)
Coneprest (Cone Mills)

SOME FINISHES USED ON COTTON

Type of Finish	Trademark	Manufacturer
Flame retardant	*Pyroset*	American Cyanamid Co.
Flame retardant	*Firestop*	Ameritex Div. of United Merchants and Manu- facturers, Inc.
Flame retardant	*Pyrovatex Cp*	Ciba-Geigy Corp.
Flame retardant	*THPC*	Hooker Chemical Co.
Flame retardant	*Fire-Guard*	Polymer Research Corp. of America
Flame retardant	*Saniflamed*	Sanitized Inc.
Shrinkage control	*Sanforized*	The Sanforized Co., Div. of Cluett, Peabody & Co.
Shrinkage control (cotton knits)	*Sanfor-Knit*	The Sanforized Co.
Shrinkage control plus crease recovery	*Sanforized-Plus*	The Sanforized Co.
Shrinkage control on durable press	*Sanforized-Plus-2*	The Sanforized Co.
Shrinkage control (cotton knits)	*Shrink-No-Mor*	The Sanforized Co.
Wash-and-wear	*Everglaze*	Joseph Bancroft & Sons
Wash-and-wear	*Minicare*	Joseph Bancroft & Sons
Wash-and-wear	*Bates Disciplined*	Bates Fabrics, Inc.
Wash-and-wear	*Coneset*	Cone Mills, Inc.
Wash-and-wear	*Wrinkl-Shed*	Dan River Mills
Wash-and-wear	*Belfast*	Deering Milliken, Inc.
Durable press (home sewn garments)	*ALMI-Set, Lifetime-Pressed*	Ameritex Div. of United Merchants and Manu- facturers, Inc.
Durable press	*Coneprest*	Cone Mills
Durable press	*Dan-Press*	Dan River Mills
Durable press	*Koratron*	Koratron Co.
Durable press (cotton knits)	*Pak-Nit RX*	Pak-Nit Compax Corp.
Durable press	*Penn Prest*	J. C. Penney Co.

SOME FINISHES USED ON COTTON (Cont.)

Type of Finish	Trademark	Manufacturer
Soil release	*Visa*	Deering Milliken, Inc.
Soil release	*Zelcon TGF*	E.I. du Pont de Nemours & Co.
Soil release	*Dual Action Scotchgard*	Chemical Div. of Minn. Mining and Manufacturing Co.
Soil release	*Rhoplex SR-488*	Rohm and Haas Co.
Oil and water repellent	*Zepel*	E.I. du Pont de Nemours & Co.
Oil and water repellent	*Scotchgard*	Chemical Div. of Minn. Mining and Manufacturing Co.

Dan-Press (Dan River)
Penn Prest (J. C. Penney Co.)
Perma-Prest (Sears, Roebuck and Co.)

Plastic coatings (acrylic resins) on draperies not only help to prevent temperature change but also cut down on the amount of soil that can penetrate the draperies and help to protect them from deterioration caused by sunlight.

Importance for the Consumer

Special finishes are directly related to the end-use requirements of the particular textile item. Their purpose is to enable the fabric to perform a certain function more effectively. They add to the aesthetic, comfort, ease-of-care, or even economic attributes of textiles. The consumer who clearly visualizes the end-use requirements for a fabric and is familiar with the special finishes available will be in a good position to match end-use and finish. For example, the consumer who is purchasing a wool blanket that will be stored for several months of the year should consider a moth-resistant finish; the homemaker selecting towels for a warm, humid climate may consider a mildew-resistant finish.

In the evaluation of a special finish, the following questions might be considered: (1) Will the finish provide the required property? For example, will a spot- and stain-resistant finish resist both waterborne and oily-type stains?

(2) Will the finish require special care in laundering, wetcleaning, or drycleaning? For example, will the resin finish discolor if the fabric is bleached with a chlorine-type bleach? Or is it a resin finish that can be chlorine-bleached?

(3) Is the finish permanent or temporary? Finishes are classified as permanent when they will successfully withstand normal wear and care for the expected life of the product.

(4) Is the finish water-soluble or solvent-soluble? A finish may be water-soluble, and, if so, is not durable in normal laundering procedures. If the finish is solvent-soluble, it will not withstand drycleaning procedures.

Some permanent finishes are water-soluble, but not solvent-soluble. Conversely, they may be solvent-soluble but not water-soluble. Most temporary finishes are both.

(5) Is the finish guaranteed to be durable to laundering, wetcleaning, or drycleaning? Or, is it semi-durable, requiring the fabric to be re-treated after garment is cleaned?

Dyes and Dyeing

Dye Classification

Dyes are soluble colored compounds which produce relatively durable permanent colors. In a dye bath, water penetrates the fiber surface particularly in the amorphous (disordered) areas of the fiber. This causes swelling of hydrophilic fibers and formation of pores within the fiber. Initially the dye molecule or ion is adsorbed on the surface of the fiber and then moves through the pores toward the center of the fiber. Dye molecules may be anchored to the fiber by electrovalent (ionic), covalent, or hydrogen bonds or other forces of a physical nature. When classified as to origin, the dyestuffs or materials that produce the color are either natural or synthetic.

Prior to 1856, only natural dyestuffs were known. For centuries, insects, plant life, shellfish, and minerals were the sources of the colors that were so necessary to the peoples of the Old World. Insects such as kermes and lac were important sources of red dyes. Indigo, madder, saffron, weld, and logwood provided the most important dyestuffs from plant life. A shellfish from the Mediterranean Sea supplied the purple color that became the symbol of royalty. This valuable dyestuff was named Tyrian purple for the city in Phoenicia credited with its discovery. Minerals were used both as sources of dyestuffs and also as a means of intensifying the dye obtained from other sources.

Since the accidental discovery of mauve in 1856, most of the dyes used for coloring fabrics are synthetic dyestuffs from *coal tar* products. Coal tar is formed during the distillation of coal, as in the manufacture of coke for use in the production of steel. Complex organic compounds are obtained in which the carbon is combined with hydrogen, nitrogen, oxygen, and sulfur.

The hydrocarbons are formed by the distillation of coal tar. At low temperatures, "light oils" which yield benzene, toluol, and xylene are formed. The "middle oils" containing phenol and related compounds are formed at slightly higher temperatures. "Heavy oils" containing naphthalene and creosote oils are collected at temperatures of 210°-270°C. The last distillate from the coal tar is the thick, paste-like "anthracene oil." Benzene, toluol, xylene, phenol, naphthalene, and anthracene are the compounds of widest use in the preparation of synthetic dyes. In recent years the petroleum industry has become a major source of most of these important compounds.

Dyes may also be classified by the nature of the way in which they are applied and the nature of the reaction necessary for color to be produced on the fabric—that is, whether the dyes will color fibers directly; whether an intermediary substance such as a mordant is required; whether the solution must be acidic or basic; and even whether the coloring substance can be applied as a solution or whether it is insoluble and must be bonded to the fiber.

The nature of the fiber to be dyed greatly influences the choice of dye.

Dyestuffs fall into the following classes according to their characteristics and their application to textiles:

Cationic or Basic Dyes

These dyes are colored salts of organic bases. The colored part of the dye molecule (the cation) is positively charged and forms electrovalent (ionic) bonds with acidic radicals of fibers such as protein, acrylic, modified nylon, and modified polyester fibers. While cationic dyes have very good colorfastness on acrylic and other modified synthetic fibers, colorfastness on protein fibers is relatively poor. Cationic dyes are noted for their brilliance of color.

Acid or Anionic Dyes

These dyes are colored salts of organic acids. The colored portion of the dye molecule (the anion) is negatively charged and forms electro-valent (ionic) bonds with the nitrogenous basic radicals of protein and nylon fibers. "Acid dye" refers to the fact that often these dyes are applied from an acid dyebath (pH 2-6). Individual dyes vary in their colorfastness to light, laundering, dry cleaning, and perspiration so that they should be selected according to the end-use of the fabric and the expected method of maintenance.

Mordant Dyes

This group of dyes includes several of the natural dyes and many of the synthetic dyes which do not have a direct affinity for the fibers but can be made to combine with metallic salts.

Mordant dyes may be applied by four different methods: (1) treating the fiber with a suitable metallic salt and then applying the dye from solution; (2) by dyeing the fiber and after-treating with a soluble metallic salt to form an insoluble lake; (3) by simultaneous application of dye and mordant so that controlled color formation occurs within the fiber; and (4) by using premetallized dyes, in which dye and mordant are reacted together before being applied to the fiber.

One of the better known mordants is chrome. Other metals include cobalt, aluminum, and nickel. Primarily such dyestuff-metal combinations are used on protein and nylon fibers, where they give excellent fastness to wet processing and to light. Copper mordants are sometimes used in the dyeing of acrylic fibers.

It is thought that both electrovalent and co-ordinate covalent bonding are involved in linking the dyestuff, metal, and fiber.

Reactive Dyes

Reactive dyes differ from other types because they form a covalent bond with the fiber. They rival vat dyes in their colorfastness to laundry and are much easier to apply. Most reactive dyes have been developed for use on cellulosic fibers, but some are available for use on protein and nylon fibers.

Direct Dyes

These are anionic dyes applied from an aqueous dyebath containing an electrolyte to cellulosic fibers and occasionally to protein and nylon fibers. Probably direct dyes are held to cellulose by hydrogen bonds and van der Waals forces. Individual dyes in the group vary considerably in fastness to light and washing so it is important that end-use be kept in mind when the dye is selected. Fastness of some dyes in this group may be improved by after-treatment with salts of copper, nickel, cobalt, or chromium, with resins, with formaldehyde, or cationic fixing agents.

Developed Direct Dyes. These dyes are similar to the direct dyes, but they must be "developed" or formed on the fiber. In the application, however, they are rendered insoluble by diazotizing the dye on the fiber and then coupling with various amines and phenols. This treatment increases the washfastness, but it may decrease the lightfastness.

Azoic Dyes

These dyes are developed on the fiber. First a colorless coupling component (e.g., a basic naphthol) solution, which is attracted to cellulose probably through hydrogen bonding, is used to impregnate cellulosic fibers. Then a solution of a colorless diazotized amine is added which reacts with the coupling component to form an insoluble colored precipitate directly within the fibers. These dyes produce a degree of fastness that is surpassed only by the vat dyes. Azoic dyes are fast to washing, acids, alkalies, chlorine, and cross-dyeing. Being developed on the surface, they have a tendency to crock. In addition, pastel shades often have poor light-fastness.

Vat Dyes

Consumers often demand vat-dyed fabrics because the colorfastness of vat dyes ranges from good to excellent. Vat dyes may be divided into two chemical groups—(1) anthraquinone dyes and (2) indigoid dyes—but the groups are alike in that the dyes are insoluble in water and go into solution only when they are reduced to their leuco compounds which are soluble in caustic alkalies. They are then reoxidized by air or by an oxidizing agent. It has been suggested that substantivity to fibers depends upon the planarity of the leuco form of the dye molecule which allows it to approach within the range of action of hydrogen bonding and/or van der Waals forces. Vat dyes are used primarily on cellulosic fibers, particularly cotton. Some may be used for synthetic fibers. However, the high alkalinity necessary to dissolve them restricts their use on protein fibers. The continuous Pad-steam process is faster than other processes so that fibers are less likely to be harmed by alkali, and better distribution of dye may occur. Fabric is treated with a fine suspension of the insoluble form, dried, padded with alkali and a reducing agent, steamed to reduce and fix the dye, and finally finished off in a soaping and rinsing range.

Sulfur Dyes

These dyes contain sulfur linkages within their molecules. Sulfur dyes resemble vat dyes in that they are insoluble in water and are applied in an alkaline solution which dissolves the reduced form. Subsequently, they are oxidized on exposure to air or oxidizing agents to the insoluble colored form in the fiber. In some sulfur dyes, the sulfur is slowly oxidized to sulfuric acid on storage and thus some dyed fabrics may be harmed. These dyes are used primarily on cellulosic fibers and produce a wide range of rather dull colors and include a few blues, browns, blacks, greens, maroons, oranges, and yellows. They are quite fast to washing and are used for fabrics that require frequent and hard washing. They have no fastness to chlorine and vary to fastness to perspiration, acids, alkalies, and light.

Disperse Dyes

The poor affinity of acetate for most dyes used for cottons and rayons was a great problem to the dye industry. A similar difficulty was encountered later with nylon, polyester, and acrylic fibers. It was found that certain insoluble azo and anthraquinone dyes can be kept in colloidal suspension by sulfonated oils or soaps. During dyeing, a dispersed dye is adsorbed by the fiber and then diffuses into the fiber, forming a solid solution. The thermosol process involves padding a disperse dye suspension into the fabric and passing the fabric into a heat zone where the dye is fixed in the fibers in seconds.

It is now possible to dye acetates, nylons, and polyesters in a range of colors with good fastness to light, washing, and perspiration. There is not, however, the wide range of colors with superior fastness that is found in the vat dyes. The susceptibility of acetates to fume-fading is still a problem that requires considerable attention to the selection and application of the dyes

which are known to be resistant and, frequently, to the finish treatments that will guarantee satisfactory fastness.

Pigments

This group of coloring agents differs from dyes, since pigments are not soluble in the media used in their application and usually have little affinity for fibers. The finely ground particles must be bonded to the fibers by means of synthetic resins or other film-forming materials.

Pigments are used primarily for dyeing and printing cotton and rayon but are also used on glass and some thermoplastic fibers. Satisfactory performance depends upon the property of the pigment and the method of binding the color to the fabric. Some pigments have excellent washfastness, others can be drycleaned only. They are usually fast to light, acids, and alkalis. Since they are applied to the surface, crocking and lack of resistance to rubbing are often encountered.

Other Dyes

With the advent of the various man-made fibers, there has arisen a need for dyestuffs which can be applied to these new fibers. Many of these dyes are modifications of the existing types. All of these dyes are usually developed so they will attach chemically to specific fibers. They offer comparatively good colorfastness.

Dyeing Processes

Solution Dye

Some man-made fibers may be dyed by the addition of the coloring matter to the solution before the filament is formed. This process results in excellent colorfastness, but it does not leave the manufacturer the same flexibility for final design that he has if the final choice of color or design is made later in the manufacturing.

Fiber Dye (or Stock Dye)

The fibers are dyed before the yarns are spun and woven into a fabric. In felts, the fibers are dyed before they are felted.

Yarn Dye

The yarns are dyed before they are woven into checks, plaids, stripes, or herringbone designs. The use of one colored yarn in the warp or lengthwise direction of a fabric and other colored yarn in the crosswise direction produces a changeable or iridescent effect.

Piece Dye

In piece dye, cloth is dyed after fabrication. This method is the easiest and cheapest but does not always provide thorough penetration of the dyestuff.

Cross Dye. Fabric of two or more fibers is placed in a dye bath containing two or more different dyes. Each fiber will be dyed by the dye for which it has an affinity.

Solid Dye. Fabric from one fiber is dyed one color.

Union Dye. This technique mixes dyes for fabrics made from two or more fibers so that the fibers will dye the same color.

Factors That Relate to Colorfastness

There are many factors that influence the fastness of the dyestuffs used today. Consumer demands for fabrics with excellent fastness properties are of great concern to the fabric manufacturer and to the dye industry. Perhaps the factor of greatest importance is the interest of the manufacturer in the selection of dyestuffs and the research in methods of application that will assure excellent performance in use. Many factors that must be considered by the manufacturer and finisher are of little concern to the consumer. However, an acquaintance with the following factors contributes to an understanding of the problems involved in obtaining colorfastness: (1) The chemical structure of the fiber to be dyed dictates the types of dyes used. Protein fibers may be dyed readily with either acid or basic dyes. Cellulose fibers are much more satisfactorily dyed with direct cotton dyes, azoic dyes, and vat and sulfur dyes. Thermoplastic fibers which do not absorb moisture require dyestuffs that either dissolve in the fibers or unite chemically with them.

(2) The chemical structure of the organic compounds must have a molecular arrangement that will enable them to absorb portions of the visible region of the electromagnetic spectrum. The substrate fabric reflects the rays that are not absorbed. Some colored materials may be converted into dyes by the introduction of salt-forming or other chemically reactive groups.

These are known as auxochromes and are represented by groups such as the amine group (NH_2), sulfonic acid (HSO_3), and the hydroxyl group (OH). These groups also give water solubility to the dye and affect the intensity or brilliance of the color.

(3) Other chemical substances are also frequently added to the bath to color fabrics successfully. *Exhausting agents* slow the dyeing process or decrease the amount of exhaustion producing a more level or uniform dyeing. *Oxidizing* and *reducing agents* regulate the amount of oxygen needed to produce the colors.

(4) Various methods of applying dyes require extra processes to fix the colors permanently. Mordanting, diazotizing and developing, and after-treating with metal salts, resins, or formaldehyde are some of the processes used.

Colorfastness Properties

Dyes are generally considered fast when they resist the deteriorating influences to which they will be subjected in the use for which the fabric is intended. Through numerous technical committees the American Association of Textile Chemists and Colorists has developed laboratory test procedures which indicate the fastness of the colors and predict their performance in use.

Fastness to *light* is a quality of importance to practically all fabrics and is of particular importance to those which are to be used for curtains, draperies, and other home furnishings. Fastness to light is often influenced by the temperature and humidity prevailing at the time of exposure. The Fade-Ometer is a standardized testing device which measures the fastness to light and shows anticipated changes.

Since almost all fabrics must withstand cleansing, colorfastness to *washing* and to *dry-cleaning* are important. Dyes must be chosen both for the fiber on which they are to be used and for the expected cleansing to be given the fabric. Mild laundering tests are used for colorfastness on delicate fabrics while more rigorous washing tests are used to determine the colorfastness on cotton and linen fabrics. Even more severe tests are established for those fabrics which must be laundered commercially.

Colorfastness tests closely related to the wash tests are those which show the resistance to *bleeding,* and those indicating the fastness to *ironing* and to *dry-* and *wet-pressing.* Fastness to *acids* and *alkalies* is also important for those fabrics that must be cleansed in commercial laundries and drycleaning establishments.

Fastness to *perspiration* is another factor of importance in wearing apparel. For greatest satisfaction, there should be no change in the color itself nor should there be any staining of suit linings or undergarments.

Fastness to *crocking* or *rubbing* is important in both apparel fabrics and those used for upholstery. Poor fastness to crocking is likely to be found with chrome dyes, basic dyes, heavy vat, and azoic dyes. Tests made with the Crockmeter aid in picking out those dyes which are likely to rub off onto white or lightly colored materials.

Fastness to *fumes* is of particular importance when related to the fastness of acetates. Although cases of fumes affecting other fibers have been known, acetates have been most affected by the oxides of nitrogen in the atmosphere, produced by the combustion of coal gas, oil burners, arc lamps, or by air passing over hot surfaces. Not all acetate dyes are affected by fumes. Those dyes that are diazotized and developed are most resistant while the amino anthraquinones are most sensitive. The increasing pollution of our atmosphere has caused failures in other kinds of dyes. Considerable research to overcome these failures is under way at the present time.

Fastness to *sea water* is important for some textile products, such as bathing suits, uniforms, flags, and sporting goods. Treatment with fairly strong solutions of salt water forms the basis of tests used for this characteristic.

Fabric Design

The two broad areas of fabric design are *structural design* and *applied decoration*.

Structural designs are achieved in the construction of the fabric by (1) combining yarns to make a particular design; (2) introducing novelty-type yarns; (3) combining colored yarns to create a particular effect; (4) using yarns with special properties; (5) making woven designs through the use of special looms such as the dobby and Jacquard; (6) introducing extra yarn or yarns to form a design on the background weave; and (7) varying knitting designs.

Applied decorative designs are those that are applied to the surface of the fabric by (1) printing, (2) embossing, (3) adding a design in relief, or (4) using chemical reactions.

Structural Design

Most of the true structural designs are permanent. A damask tablecloth, for example, will never lose its design, though of course its beauty, luster, and colorfastness will depend on the quality of fabric construction, yarn, and dye. A woven iridescent fabric will keep its changeable effect as long as the fabric lasts if the dyes are colorfast. Various methods of achieving structural design are briefly described here. For more detailed information see sections on yarns and fabric construction.

Yarn Type and Arrangement

Combining Yarns. The combination of different types of yarns in a specified arrangement may be used to create designs. For example, bengaline is a firmly woven, ribbed-weave fabric made of single yarns in the warp and of heavy ply yarns in the filling. A basket weave fabric is made by weaving two or more yarns together in both warp and filling.

Spacing Yarns. Design effects may be obtained by skipping spaces in either the warp or filling direction. This arrangement of yarns produces sheer stripes in the fabric.

Yarns with Special Properties. Puckered stripes in seersucker are made by alternating groups of warp yarns with loose and tight tensions, thus giving lengthwise pucker stripes in the areas of loose tension. A method that closely resembles plissé or seersucker uses yarns with greater shrinkage potential alternated with regular yarns. The shrinkage produced in a heat-setting process causes the high shrinkage yarns to shorten and thus also causes the alternate yarns to pucker. This method could be used in either the lengthwise or crosswise direction.

Novelty Yarns. Novelty yarns (such as slub, bouclé, or other core-and-effect yarns) and textured yarns may be woven or knitted into the fabric to create a structural design that serves a useful as well as aesthetic purpose. For example, nylon and rayon yarns coated with tiny glass beads may be woven into a fabric. Under ordinary light, the yarns are unchanged. Seen in a strong light, they glow. Such yarns have important safety uses.

Colored Yarns. Variation in the arrangement of colored yarns may be used to create design. Alternated groups of colored yarn are used to form stripes, checks, and plaids. Warp and filling yarns in contrasting colors are used to achieve iridescent fabrics, such as changeable taffeta.

Weaves and Variations

Use of Special Looms. Small, fancy, and geometrical designs are woven on the dobby loom; more elaborate designs are woven on the Jacquard loom. Examples of Jacquard-woven fabrics are brocade and damask.

Knits with Extra Yarns. (1) *Lappet designs* resemble embroidery but are formed by needles which carry extra warp yarns from side to side of the design where they are bound by filling yarns. Long floats between designs are cut away, thus leaving the cut ends on the same side of the fabric as the design. Looms equipped for lappet weaving are not now in general use. (2) *Swivel designs* are woven with extra filling yarns, each carried by a special swivel shuttle around several warp yarns. The cut ends of the yarns in the pattern appear on the wrong side of the fabric. True swivel figures are usually securely anchored to the ground, but clipped spot designs may be easily pulled out. These designs are made by weaving extra filling yarns in spots across the fabric and cutting the loose floats at the ends of each figure.

Knits and Variations

Attractive structural designs can also be formed by use of different knitting techniques and patterns. Variations of the basic stitches and the use of different knitting machines make it possible to create fabrics with a wide variety of structural designs.

Applied Decoration

Printing

Colors or chemicals are applied in patterns to the surface of the fabric to achieve decorative designs. This is called printing. Examples of various processes are:

Blotch Printing. The ground or base area around the design is covered with color; the detail colors of the design are applied by different rolls or screens. This is a method of direct printing; however, the appearance is similar to a discharge print fabric.

Burnt-out Printing. A fabric composed of yarns of at least two fibers is printed with a solvent or an agent capable of destroying one of the fibers. As one of the fibers is removed (burnt out) in the area where the solvent or agent was printed, a lacy or sheer-and-heavy design is created. This method may also be used to make eyelet designs.

Direct (or Application) Printing. A process in which colors for the design are applied directly to the fabric as the fabric passes between a large cylinder and engraved rollers. The rollers transfer color directly to fabric. Both background color and design may be printed in the same operation. Each color requires a separate roller. This process is also known as *cylinder, calender,* or *roller printing.*

Discharge (or Extract) Printing. The fabric is piece-dyed; then the dye is removed in selected areas by printing chemicals that reduce or remove the dye as the design is printed. The result may be a white design on a colored fabric or a colored design imprinted at the same time the selected areas of color are removed to form the design.

Duplex Printing. Designs are printed on the face and back of the fabric in two distinct operations on both sides of the fabric. The designs and colors may be identical or different. Identical designs may give the effect of a woven design.

Lacquer Printing. Insoluble pigments are mixed with a lacquer carrier to form a printing paste and are then applied by rollers to an already finished piece of goods, for example, a taffeta or a faille. The design does not stand out in relief on the surface of the fabric. This type of print is difficult to distinguish from a pigment-resin print.

Lacquer Stencil Printing. In lacquer stencil printing, insoluble, finely ground pigments are mixed with a binder and a thickener to form a printing paste. This is then applied to the fabric in a variety of designs. The design stands in relief to the background fabric and looks like paint designs.

Overprinting. Technically, overprinting is direct or application printing. The design is printed over other colors already on the fabric. Overprinting can tone down certain vivid colors or alter shades of colors.

Photographic Printing. Photoengraved rollers transfer the design (a photographic image) to the fabric.

Pigment-Resin Printing. An insoluble pigment is mixed with a resin binder and thickener to form a printing paste. The paste is then applied to the fabric from engraved rollers. The printed fabric is treated at a high temperature to cure the resin binder. The design does not stand in relief on the surface of the fabric.

Plissé Printing. A process used to create a crinkled or puckered surface. A cotton fabric is passed between rollers that permit a caustic solution to come in contact with certain areas of the fabric. The solution shrinks those areas, and the unprinted portions pucker. A variation of this method uses a resisting solution to protect parts of the fabric, and a caustic bath then shrinks the unprotected areas. Fabrics of other fibers may also be given a plissé effect by use of selected chemicals.

Resist Printing. In one method a chemical or substance is printed in a design on a white or light-colored fabric. When the fabric is then piece-dyed and washed, the resisted patterns stay uncolored against a colored background. The fabric may then be direct-printed to color the blank areas. Or the fabric may be printed with a dye paste that resists another dye when over-printed.

Roller Printing. See **Direct Printing.**

Screen Printing. The background of the design is blocked out with various materials on a screen of silk or nylon. The untreated areas of the screen allow the dye to pass through onto the fabric. A separate screen is used for each color of the pattern.

Stencil Printing. This is a type of resist printing in which the part of the design to resist the dye is covered with paper or metal; open areas of the stencil allow the dye to be applied to the fabric.

Vigoureux (or Melange) Printing. This method is used mainly on wool for creating greys and salt-and-pepper effects in men's suiting. A dye is printed in crosswise stripes on slivers. When the sliver is processed into yarn, the colors appear as small spots and produce a tweedy effect or blend to give a grey tone, depending upon amount of processing.

Warp Printing. The warp yarns are printed with the design after they have been set up on the warp beam of the loom. The printed warp yarns are woven with a plain-colored filling yarn. A shadowy or muted design is achieved.

Surface Designs Other Than Printing

Fabric decoration may also be created by surface-applied design other than printing. These methods of design application may be used on both dyed and printed fabrics and on various types of fabric constructions. Examples are:

Embossed Designs. The fabric is pressed between engraved rollers to produce a design on the surface of the fabric. (Embossed designs may be found on cotton or silk and on rayon, acetate, and other man-made fiber fabrics of many different constructions.) There are two methods for embossing designs on fabrics: (1) By the *mechanical* method, the design is pressed into a fabric under conditions of heat, moisture, and steam. (2) By the *chemical* method, the design is pressed into a fabric that has been pretreated with a resin. Embossed designs are durable when they are properly executed on fabrics of thermoplastic fibers or those pretreated with a heat-setting resin.

Embroidered Designs. Fabric is embroidered by hand or machine in a repeated design.

Flocked Designs. A fabric is first printed with an adhesive, then dusted with flocks (short fibers, short hairs, or metallic particles) which adhere to the adhesive, forming a design that stands in relief to the surface of the fabric. Some flocked designs are made by use of an electrostatic charge that pulls the flock upright through the fabric so that flock stands perpendicular to the surface.

Glued Designs. Various types of materials may be glued to the fabric to form a design in relief to the surface. For example, felt cutout designs may be glued to a felt skirt. Chenille or sequin dots may be glued to a fabric surface. In some instances, the adhesive used is solvent-soluble, and the design comes off in drycleaning.

Hand-Painted Designs. The design may be painted on a section of a garment before the garment is made or may be applied to a finished item. For example: hand-painted designs on blouses; painted designs on ties. Some painted designs dryclean satisfactorily; others do not.

Moiré. A watered or wavered effect on fabrics, produced by passing the fabric between engraved rollers. The crushed and uncrushed parts of the design reflect light differently. Moiré designs may be found on cotton, silk, and man-made fiber fabrics, such as rayon and acetate, of many different constructions. If the finish is to be durable, the fabric must contain thermoplastic fibers or resins. *Bar moiré* is the process used for almost all moirés now on the market. It is a mechanical method that uses moisture, heat, and pressure. Design forms in wavy bars.

Importance for the Consumer

The importance of design to the consumer is primarily aesthetic. Design may make a fabric more pleasing in appearance and more becoming to the wearer since the fabric is more decorative than it would be without the design. Design is also an important style consideration.

Permanence of the design and the effect that its application may have had or will have on the base fabric need to be considered. For example, certain dyes may, through photosynthesis due to exposure to sunlight, develop chemicals that can damage the fabric. Novelty or textured yarns may be more easily snagged and thus damage the appearance or durability of the fabric. From experience and care in buying, the consumer can judge the permanence of some designs; for most decisions, however, he will need to rely on the manufacturer's label or information from the retailer. With new finishing techniques and products, it is possible to produce very permanent surface-design effects.

Fabric Definitions

The definitions given here include a description of the distinctive characteristics of the fabric as well as other information which will help to identify it. Some of the ways the various fabrics are commonly used are included; however, the examples are not intended to be all-inclusive. As new fibers, yarns, and blends are developed, they extend or alter the ways the fabrics are used and sometimes the character of the traditional fabric. There are an increasing number of fabrics known to the consumer by the trade or brand name rather than by the traditional fabric name; therefore, some brand names have also been included.

Alpaca. A fabric made from a wool-like fiber derived from domesticated llama. Alpaca is usually available in a plain-weave fabric which is fine, soft, and luxurious. Like mohair, the fiber is stiff, and though the fabric is soft, it has a crisp hand. Fabrics with the characteristic crisp, wiry hand of alpaca, currently made of blends of rayon and other man-made fibers, are sometimes called alpaca.

Awning Cloth. Durable canvas or duck, made with a plain weave. This fabric is used in solid colors or in woven or painted stripes for awnings, beach and lawn umbrellas, outdoor furniture covers, and luggage.

Balbriggan. A lightweight circular knit fabric made with plain stitch. Used for underwear, sweaters, gloves.

Barathea. A fabric with a characteristic granular textured effect because of the short broken ribs in the filling direction. It is a rich, soft, fine fabric which may be made of silk, rayon, or acetate warp with a worsted filling. Used in neckties and dress goods.

Batiste. General term for soft, lightweight, thin fabric made in plain weave of cotton, or man-made fibers such as rayon. Used for dresses, blouses, handkerchiefs, and infants' wear. Batiste is the finest and softest of the related group of plain-weave cloths such as lawn. Corset batiste is quite different, is generally very firm and heavy, and may have an overall Jacquard or dobby pattern.

Bedford Cord. A firm warpwise ribbed fabric. Stuffing yarns are introduced to make a raised cord. Used for coats, suits, slacks, uniforms. Heavier qualities of this fabric are used in draperies and slipcovers.

Bengaline. Firmly woven ribbed-weave fabric made of single yarns in the warp and heavy ply yarns in the filling. Warp yarns may be of man-made fibers or silk and the filling yarns of cotton, wool, or man-made fibers alone, or in combinations. Ribs are slightly heavier and rounder than in poplin; more distinct than in faille. Fabric is usually stiffer than poplin or faille. Used in dresses, coatings, ribbons.

Bird's-eye. A figure-weave fabric. The figure forms a diamond with a dot in the center. Used in dresses, diapers, and household items.

Blends. The combination of two or more types of fibers in one yarn used in various fabric constructions.

Bolivia. Fabric with a silky, thick, long pile which is woven and then cut to give a pebbled, cord, or ridge effect. In some fabrics the ridges go up and down; in other fabrics the ridges may go diagonally across the fabric. Usually made of wool; may contain alpaca or mohair.

Bouclé. Term applied to a variety of knitted and woven fabric constructions, from lightweight dress fabrics to heavy coating fabrics made of bouclé yarn. Regardless of weight or construction, fabrics are distinguished by small spaced loops on their surfaces. May be made from either natural or man-made fibers or mixtures of both.

Broadcloth. Term used to describe several dissimilar fabrics made with different fibers, weaves, and finishes. They may be defined as follows:

Broadcloth made from wool or wool mixed with man-made fibers. Fine, open twill-weave fabrics that are "fulled," napped, sheared, and dampened. The nap is then permanently laid down in one direction. The weave cannot be seen on the right side of the fabric. This gives the fabric its characteristic smooth, lustrous, fine velvet-like texture. Chiffon broadcloth is a lightweight dress fabric with a high luster. Coating and suiting broadcloths are heavier.

Broadcloth made from spun man-made fiber yarns. To form the rib in this fabric, a number of filling yarns may be woven as one yarn, or a heavier filling yarn may be used. This type of broadcloth has the finest rib of all ribbed-weave fabrics.

Broadcloth made from silk or filament-type synthetic yarns. Fabrics are woven in a plain weave with a fine crosswise rib obtained by using a heavier filling than warp yarn.

Broadcloth made from cotton and spun man-made fiber yarns. Fine fabrics with a slight rib in the filling direction.

Brocade. A rich-appearing fabric woven on a Jacquard loom. Has a prominent and raised design; face of fabric may be distinguished from the back. May be made of the natural or man-made fibers. In some fabrics, a gold or silver yarn may be introduced to form the design.

Brocatelle. Tightly woven and stiff, elaborate fabric made with a Jacquard figure weave. Originally made to look like tooled leather. The design, formed by the warp yarns, stands in high relief from the ground. The area that is not raised is backed by extra yarns. Used chiefly for slipcovers, upholstery, and wall coverings.

Buckram. Term used to describe three types of fabrics.

A heavily sized and stiffened fabric is made by gluing two fabrics together. One is a low-count, open, plain-weave fabric, the other a much finer plain-weave fabric.

A single strong linen fabric is stiffened with flour, paste, China clay, and glue.

A cotton scrim is given a stiff finish with a nondurable size. Used for interlinings, bookbindings, millinery.

Bunting. Loosely woven plain-weave fabric made of cotton, wool, or man-made fibers. Used for flags and banners.

Burlap. Very coarse, heavy, plain-weave fabric made of cotton, jute, or hemp. Used chiefly for backs of floor coverings or furniture covering and bagging, but may also be used natural, dyed, or printed for clothing, draperies, and wall hangings.

Butcher Rayon. A coarse, crash-like rayon fabric made to resemble the original butcher linen. A Federal Trade Commission ruling prohibits the use of the word "linen" on this type of fabric.

Calico. Originally lightweight plain-weave cotton cloth, made in Calcutta, India. The name today refers more to a type of design in the print rather than to a given fabric construction. Print cloths may be called calico when printed with a small overall floral design in dark or bright colors.

Camel's Hair. Fabrics made from wool-like hair obtained from the camel. Genuine fabrics are very expensive and not too common. They are soft, silky, and luxurious. Some fabrics combine camel hair with wool.

Canvas. Heavy, closely woven, plain-weave fabric that is rather stiff. Made of cotton or linen or man-made fibers in many weights. Uses of canvas range from sails and awnings to slipcover and lining fabrics.

Casement Cloth. Term applied to a class of lightweight, sheer openwork, or opaque fabrics used for curtains.

Cashmere. Wool-like hair fiber from the cashmere goat. Fabrics using this fiber alone, or in combination with wool, are often called cashmere. Typical are the cashmere shawls from northern India.

Cassimere. Closely woven 2 x 2 twill fabric made of wool. It is fulled and sheared to make a smooth, somewhat lustrous surface texture. Chief use is for men's suits and trousers.

Cavalry Twill. Very firmly woven, hard-surfaced fabric, recognizable by its pronounced double twill. Spaced diagonal lines go from left to right and can be seen on the back of the fabric. Used for riding habits, sportswear, uniforms.

Challis. Extremely soft, lightweight, plain- or twill-weave fabric made of wool, cotton, or man-made fibers. Usually printed with a small floral pattern. Used for dresses, blouses, negligees, men's ties and shirts, draperies, linings.

Chambray. Plain-weave fabric distinguished by a white frosted appearance achieved by use of a white yarn in the filling, a colored yarn in the warp. Used for linings, women's blouses and dresses, and men's shirts.

Cheesecloth. A very loosely woven, plain-weave cotton fabric. It may be used for curtains, costumes, cleaning cloths.

Chenille. Term applied to a type of yarn and to a fabric woven with a chenille yarn. The yarn is covered with short cut fibers or pile. Chenille yarns are used in both knitted and woven fabrics. The fabric is used chiefly in making lounging garments, bedspreads, rugs.

Cheviot. Originally a fabric made of the coarse wool of sheep raised in the Cheviot Hills of North England. Today it is a term used to describe medium- to heavyweight fabrics made of wool, wool and cotton, spun man-made yarns, or entirely of cotton. Weave may be plain, or twill. The fabric is "fulled" for compactness, then napped to produce a rough, shaggy surface texture which is its distinguishing characteristic.

Chiffon. Term used to describe many sheer, plain-weave fabrics made of fine, highly twisted, strong yarn. May be made of silk, wool, or a man-made fiber. The term is used before names of fabrics to indicate a lightness of weight, as chiffon taffeta, chiffon satin, chiffon velvet. Some chiffon constructions made of fibers other than silk are sized with a water-soluble size to give them the hand and feel of silk.

China Silk. Lightweight, soft, plain-weave silk fabric used for lingerie and linings of dresses and soft suits.

Chinchilla. Term used to describe a variety of wool and cotton fabrics made of twill double cloth or knitted constructions. Fabrics are characterized by a thick, full, soft, dull, irregular surface texture resulting from curled nubs. Long, floating yarns are teaseled by a chinchilla machine to raise a long nap to the surface of the fabric. The nap is then rubbed into small rounded, curled tufts or nubs. The fabric is used chiefly for coats. The term "chinchilla" also refers to fur of a rodent.

Chintz. Term applied to a large group of gaily printed or solid colored, highly glazed cotton fabrics. High-quality fabrics are made of a hard twisted warp yarn and a coarser, slackly twisted filling yarn and are firmly woven. Some of the fabrics are fully glazed; some are semi-glazed. The two methods of producing a glazed finish on this group of fabrics are: (1) *nondurable*, a fabric that has been given a wax or starch finish and then pressed between hot rollers to produce a high luster; and (2) *durable*, a fabric that has been treated with a resin under patented methods that produce a high luster.

Coated Fabrics

Simulated leather. Term used to describe a thermosetting-resin-coated fabric that has the look, feel, and pliability of leather. Base fabric may be knitted or woven of a variety of fabric constructions.

Reflective linings. Conventional suit and coat lining fabrics such as satin, taffeta, and twill- and plain-weave lining fabrics and conventional cotton drapery linings such as sateen, brocades, print cloth (a plain-weave fabric of cotton or blends) are coated on one side with aluminum flakes in a resin binder. Both types may be sold under various trademark names.

Opaque linings. Conventional drapery fabrics such as sateen or print cloth are coated on one side with a vinyl resin material to make the fabric opaque.

Coated outerwear fabrics. Medium-weight fabrics, usually cotton, are coated on the back of

Coated Fabrics (Continued)

the fabric with a rubberized coating or a vinyl coating to make the fabric weather-resistant.

Coated rainwear fabrics. Lightweight fabrics of cotton, silk, rayon, nylon, or polyester are thinly coated on the back of the fabric to impart water-resistance to the fabric.

Flocked fabrics. A flocked fabric is made by binding small particles of fibers (called flock) to the entire surface of a woven fabric.

Flocked velvet. A flocked velvet is made by binding small particles of fibers (called flock) to the entire surface of a taffeta fabric. The finished fabric looks very much like a woven velveteen or velvet.

Metallic-plated fabrics. Nylon or acetate tricot knit fabrics are coated on one side with silver or gold particles in a resin binder.

Corduroy. A cut filling-pile fabric with lengthwise ridges or wales that may vary from fine (pinwale) to wide wales. Extra filling yarns float over a number of warp yarns that form either a plain- or twill-weave ground. After the fabric is woven the floating yarns are cut, the pile brushed and singed to produce a clear cord effect. The back of corduroy is slightly napped. Originally a cotton fabric, but today may be made of man-made fibers such as rayon, polyester, or acrylic.

Covert. A medium- to heavyweight twill-weave fabric. Distinguishing characteristic is mottled or flecked appearance achieved by use of a solid colored filling yarn and a two-ply warp yarn of white and colored single yarns. Usually made of wool or cotton but may be made of man-made fibers. Used for coats, sportswear, suits.

Crash. A rather loosely woven fabric of irregular yarns of cotton, linen, rayon, or jute. Made in various weights. May be dyed or printed. Used for upholstery, draperies, slipcovers. Lightweight crash may be used for dresses for casual wear.

Crepe. Term used to describe a large class of fabrics made of a plain weave or modification which is distinguished by a grainy or crinkled surface. Highly twisted yarns are used in either the warp or filling directions or both. According to their construction, crepe fabrics may be classified as follows: (1) *Warp crepes* have high-twist yarns in warp direction only. Bemberg sheers and some wool crepes are of this type. (2) *Filling crepes* have high-twist yarns in the filling direction only. The use of many more warp than filling yarns gives these fabrics a characteristic crosswise rib. French, flat, bark crepes, and crepe de Chine are examples of filling crepes. (3) *Balanced crepes* have high-twist yarns in both warp and filling directions. Examples of balanced crepes include chiffon, georgette, triple sheer, and semi-sheer.

Different effects also may be achieved by the way the yarns are twisted. Crepes made with a satin, twill, or Jacquard weave usually have another name.

Crepe fabrics range from the very fine, almost smooth surfaces to very pronounced definite heavy crepe textured surfaces. Crepe fabrics include:

Canton crepe. Originally made in China, from which it has derived its name. Soft, lustrous, similar to crepe de Chine but heavier and more textured. A predominant, heavy creped filling yarn forms a crosswise rib. This is achieved by the alternate use of six or more filling yarns with an **S** twist and six or more filling yarns with the **Z** twist.

Chiffon crepe. See **Chiffon.**

Crepe-back satin. See **Satin.**

Crepe de Chine. A soft, thin but opaque lightweight fabric with a crepe surface. Silk crepe de Chine is woven with the natural gum. The crepe effect is achieved during the degumming process.

Crepon. Originally a wool fabric, but today may be made of silk or rayon. A heavy crepe fabric with a wavy lengthwise rib formed by a thicker, alternately twisted crepe warp yarn.

Flat crepe. Smooth, soft fabric that has a less crinkled surface than most crepes.

Marocain crepe. Heavy crepe fabric with a slightly wavy and rather heavy filling rib.

Plissé or crinkle crepes. Many crepes fall in this class. They may be produced by chemical treatment in the fabric.

Crinoline. Originally a linen and horsehair fabric used for linings and interlinings. The horsehair provided required stiffness. Today crinoline describes a dull, low-count, coarse, medium-weight fabric that is sized to give it stiffness. The size may be of two types: (1) *non-durable* which is a starch finish applied to a cotton fabric; and (2) *durable* which is a resin finish that gives the fabric stiffness.

Damask. A firm, lustrous, reversible fabric woven on the Jacquard loom. May be made of cotton, linen, silk, wool, or man-made fiber yarn. The design is flat, thus differing from a brocade. Three types of damask fabrics are: (1) the light-weight type used for table linens, (2) the medium weight type used for wearing apparel, and (3) the heavyweight type used for drapery and upholstery fabrics.

Deep-Pile Fabrics. Deep-pile fabrics are made with either a knit or woven back and with a pile of varying density and depth. Some are treated or printed to resemble fur and are referred to as fake fur or imitation fur fabrics. The back may be of cotton or man-made fiber and the pile of man-made fiber.

Denim. A twill-weave fabric made of coarse, hard-twisted yarns, usually cotton. The warp yarn may be colored, and the filling yarn white; however, the fabric may also be piece-dyed. It is calendered to give it a smooth surface. Scrubbed denim is slightly napped and has a worn appearance. Used for slipcovers, draperies, sportswear, children's clothing.

Dimity. Sheer, crisp plain-weave fabric with corded stripe or check effect. Mercerized to give smoothness and luster. Used for dresses, blouses, curtains, bedspreads.

Doeskin. Very fine wool fabric, napped and finished to give it high luster. Looks like soft-finished leather. Used for suits, sportswear, coats.

Dotted Swiss. Open-weave, sheer, crisp, plain-weave fabric with woven or flocked dots. Used for dresses, blouses, curtains.

Double-cloth. Two separate fabrics, woven at the same time, are joined in weaving through the use of binding threads. Different colors and patterns on each side make fabric reversible.

Drill. A heavy, firm cotton twill-weave that is sized and pressed to make a compact fabric. Khaki cloth is a drill in khaki color. Middy twill or jeans are drill. Drill is also used in sportswear, curtains, slipcovers.

Duck. Very durable, closely-woven fabric, usually made of cotton. (See **Awning Cloth** and **Canvas.**)

Duvetyn. Name comes from the French *duvet* meaning "down." A soft, silky, velvet-like fabric. May be made of wool, silk, cotton, or man-made fibers or a mixture of two. Fibers are raised to the surface of the fabric by emery rollers, then sheared, singed, and brushed for a smooth, lustrous surface.

End-and-End Cloth. Closely woven plain-weave fabric, usually cotton, with a fine colored stripe or pin check made by alternating a white and colored yarn in the warp or in both the warp and filling. Used for men's shirts.

Eponge. A loosely woven plain-weave fabric made with a bouclé yarn. Name is derived from a French word meaning "sponge." Used in dresses, suits, draperies.

Faille. Soft, yet firm ribbed-weave fabric made of cotton, silk, or man-made fibers alone or in combination. Compared to grosgrain, faille is softer and has larger, flattened, almost inconspicuous ribs. Used for coats, dresses, handbags.

Felt. A heavy compact material made from wool, hair, fur, or certain synthetic fibers. *Unwoven* or *pressed felt* is made by a suitable combination of pressure, heat, moisture, and chemical action that interlocks the unspun fibers. *Woven felt* uses spun fibers, is first woven, and then subjected to a felting operation that gives the fabric the characteristic matted felt nap. Grades and weights of felt range from very light to very heavy. *Net-based felt* is a lightweight felt with a nylon net base running through the center of the cloth and wool and rayon fibers felted to both sides of the netting.

Flannel. A large group of napped plain- or twill-weave fabrics made of cotton, wool, or man-made fibers. Fabrics vary in closeness or firmness of weave, and degree of napping. For example, a French flannel is a very fine twill-weave fabric, slightly napped on the right side only, whereas a suede flannel is napped on both sides, sheared, and the fibers pressed into the fabric, giving the appearance of a close-felted fabric. *Viyella* flannel (Wm. Hollins & Company, Inc.) is slightly napped twill-weave flannel made of part lamb's wool and part cotton. It is treated so that it is guaranteed not to shrink.

Flannelette. Soft, plain- or twill-weave cotton fabric lightly napped on one side. May be dyed solid colors or printed. Used for lounging and sleeping garments and shirts.

Foulard. Lightweight silk, rayon, cotton, or wool fabric characterized by its twill weave and its soft finish and feel. It has a high luster on the right side; dull on the under or reverse side. Fabric patterns range from simple polka dots to elaborate designs and are usually printed. Also made in plain or solid colors. Suitable for dresses, robes, scarves.

Frieze. Heavy, coarse, napped twill-weave fabric. Nap is rough textured, producing a hard feel. Used for coats, sport jackets. Also refers to a woven pile fabric sometimes called frisé, with a surface of uncut loops or cut and uncut loops forming a pattern. Used for upholstery.

Fur-imitation Fabrics (Fake Furs).[1] These are pile fabrics made to look like fur. Different types of *knit fabrics* fall within this classification. Among these are the following:

Knit imitation krimmer. Cotton knit back. Loops on surface may be of wool, wool and rayon, wool and acetate.

Knit fur prints. Brushed rayon knit that is printed to simulate the markings on genuine fur, such as leopard, zebra, etc.

Knit pony and mock mole. Made of a brushed knit with a long nap. The fabric is given mechanical treatment which results in markings that are characteristic of natural pony or mole fur.

---

[1] Certain animal names that are used in the description cannot be used on labels or in advertising of these products. See Textile Fiber Products Identification Act, page 95.

Fake furs also include *woven fabrics* such as the following:

Cotton velour. A cut pile cotton fabric similar to cotton velvet, but with a heavier, denser pile. It may be printed to resemble zebra, leopard, tiger, or python.

Imitation caracul. Characterized by lofty loops or curls of a thick lustrous yarn on the surface of the fabric. Loops may be of mohair, lustrous wool, or worsted; background may be of wool or cotton.

Imitation Persian paw. Cotton back, wool pile. The pile is thick, deep, lustrous, and curled and pressed into a design that resembles genuine paw fur.

Imitation broadtail. Usually cotton back, wool or man-made fiber pile. The pile is short, sleek, and flat. The fabric is given a mechanical finish which simulates genuine broadtail.

Simulated Persian lamb. This fabric may be made in either of the following ways: (1) The center or core of the curl is made of a two-ply cotton yarn. These yarns are twisted to hold acetate fibers that are curled very tightly around the center. These curls are held to a plain-weave cotton fabric with adhesive.

(2) The curled yarns are made as described above, but they are stitched to the plain-weave background fabric by means of a Schiffli embroidery machine.

Gabardine. A hard-finished, clear-surfaced twill-weave fabric made of either natural or man-made fibers. Diagonal lines are fine, close, and steep from left to right. They are more pronounced than in serge. The lines cannot be seen on the wrong side of the fabric. Widely used in men's and women's outer apparel.

Gauze. A plain-weave fabric with widely spaced yarns. Used for bandages, etc. Some weights may be stiffened for use as curtains or for other decorative or apparel purposes.

Georgette. A thin, transparent or semi-transparent, loosely woven fabric. Silk georgette has a fine crepe surface. Compared to crepe de Chine, georgette has a harder finish, is less lustrous, and is more crepey. Traditionally made of silk, georgette may also be made of man-made fibers or wool. Popularly used for blouses worn with soft, feminine-type suits.

Gingham. A light- to medium-weight closely woven plain-weave fabric made of cotton or blends of cotton and man-made fibers. Usually yarn-dyed and woven to create stripes, checks, or plaids. It is sized and calendered to a firm and lustrous finish. Used for dresses, shirts, robes, curtains, draperies, bedspreads.

Gros de Londres. Closely woven, yet lightweight ribbed-weave fabric of silk or the man-made fibers. Distinguished by its alternate heavy and fine rib. A heavy flat rib may be followed by one or more fine ribs and then another heavy rib. It has a stiffness comparable to taffeta.

Grosgrain. Hard-finished, closely woven, uniformly ribbed-weave fabric made of cotton, silk, or man-made fibers, or combinations of fibers. The crosswise ribs are heavier than in poplin and more rounded than in faille.

Hair Canvas. Interfacing materials made in various weights. Hair may be goat hair combined with other fibers such as wool, cotton, rayon, or polyester.

Hair-Fiber Fabrics. Specialty hair-fiber fabrics include a large class of dress, suit, and coating fabrics. Fibers are from fur-bearing animals, such as rabbit, beaver, mink, and Angora; and hair fibers such as guanaco, vicuña, alpaca, cashmere, camel's hair, and mohair. Hair fibers may be used alone, but more often are blended with wool or other fibers.

Herringbone. Term applied to a type of twill-weave and to the fabric. The distinguishing characteristic of the fabric is the broken twill-weave that gives a balanced zigzag effect which resembles the backbone of the herring. Used for sportswear, suits, coats.

Homespun. Coarse, plain-weave fabric, loosely woven with irregular, tightly twisted, unevenly spun yarns. Has a handwoven appearance. Used for coats, suits, sportswear, draperies, slipcovers.

Honeycomb or Waffle Cloth. The fabrics are rough-textured with a raised square or diamond-shaped pattern made by floating warp and filling yarns that form ridges along the lines of the floats. Used in dresses, bedspreads.

Hopsacking. Open basket-weave fabric made of coarse woolen or cotton yarns. Used for sportswear, draperies.

Huck or Huckaback. Linen or cotton fabric with small figure weave. The warp yarn floats on the surface, the filling yarn on the back. The fabric makes very absorbent and durable towels.

Interfacings. Woven or nonwoven fabrics used to provide firmness and shape retention in garments.

Jaspé. Plain-weave fabric made from different-colored warp yarns and a single-color filling yarn creating faint, blended, multicolored stripes. May be made of hard-twisted cotton or rayon yarns, producing a firm fabric. Used for draperies and slipcovers.

Jean. A cotton twill or chevron twill fabric similar to denim with a firm, clear-surfaced texture. Sometimes jean is called "middy twill." Used for slipcovers, workclothes, children's clothes.

Knit Fabrics. To produce a variety of knitted fabrics, manufacturers may vary the type of knitting stitch, change the fiber content of the yarns, use novelty-type yarns, or knit an extra yarn into the background fabric. Finishing techniques and printing may also be used to create certain effects and change the appearance so that a knitted fabric may look like a conventional, woven fabric. Types of knit fabrics are:

Brushed knits. Knit fabrics can be given a finishing treatment that raises the fibers to the surface of the fabric. In brushed knits, the background loops cannot be seen on the face of the fabric.

Jersey knit. A plain stitch knitted fabric which may be made circular, flat, or warp knitted. Made from cotton, wool, and man-made fibers. Used in underwear, dresses, sportswear.

Milanese. A type of warp knitted fabric with several sets of yarns forming a pronounced twill

Knit Fabrics (Continued)

rib running diagonally on the fabric. A sheer, fine fabric knitted on a Milanese machine. Used in blouses, evening-wear fabrics.

Ribbon knit. Narrow silk or man-made fiber ribbon is used instead of yarn in making the fabric, either by hand or machine. In machine ribbon knits, the background yarn may be cotton and the surface of the knit ribbon.

Suede-type knits. Knit fabrics are given a mechanical finishing treatment that raises short fibers to the surface of the fabric. Fibers are sheared and pressed into the fabric to give the appearance of suede leather. Loops of the background knit cannot be seen on the surface of the fabric. Suede-type knits may be made of wool, cotton, and man-made fibers.

Tricot. A run-resistant warp knit made with either single or double sets of yarns. Has fine, lengthwise wales on the face and crosswise ribs on the back. *Tissue tricot* is a nylon tricot made of fine yarn and given a special heat-finishing process which flattens the yarns and produces greater opacity.

Lace. There are many different kinds of machine-made laces used for all-over garment designs, insertions, flouncing, and beadings. Their distinctive feature is their bobbin construction of knotted, twisted, or looped yarns, varying from very simple and fine constructions to very coarse and complicated constructions. Terms used for parts of lace are:

A jour. The open-work design that forms the pattern.

Cordonnet. The heavy thread or yarn that outlines the design.

Ground. The inside part of the design.

Mesh. The net part made by a needle or bobbin.

Picot. The little loops on the surface of the design or along the edge of the lace.

Réseau. The background as distinguished from the prominent design.

Lamé. A fabric with metallic threads. Used for blouses, evening wear, and for decorative purposes.

Laminated Fabric. Any fabric bonded to a lightweight foam backing, or two different fabrics bonded together.

Lawn. A fine, lightweight fabric, usually cotton, linen, or blends of cotton and man-made fibers. May be given a soft or crisp finish. It is sized and calendered to give it a soft, lustrous appearance. Used for dresses, blouses, curtains, bedspreads.

Leno. Name of a weave and a lightweight, firm, open-weave fabric, made of cotton, wool, silk, or man-made fibers. Used for dresses, blouses, curtains, draperies.

Linen. Term refers to the yarn and fabric formed from the fibers of the flax plant. Fabrics are available in different weights and varieties. Types of linen fabric include *art linen, linen damask, handkerchief linen, Irish linen.* Used for wearing apparel, household articles, fancy work. The use depends on the fineness and type of linen fabric.

Mackinaw Cloth. Thick, heavy, felted, and napped wool fabric made with either a twill-weave or double-cloth construction. It is recognized by its bold plaid designs. May have cotton and rayon warp in lower-priced fabrics. Used for jackets, blankets, shirts.

Madras. A fine fabric that is one of the oldest staples of the cotton trade. There are two types.

Shirting madras. A finely woven, soft, plain- or Jacquard-weave fabric. A stripe runs in the lengthwise direction and Jacquard or dobby patterns are woven in the background. Some madras is made with woven checks and cords. Used for blouses, dresses, shirts.

Authentic **India madras** is handwoven from cotton yarns dyed with native vegetable colorings and resembles gingham. Designs are usually rather large bold plaids that soften in color as the dyes fade and bleed.

Marocain. See **Crepe, Marocain.**

Marquisette. Sheer but relatively strong leno-weave fabric of cotton or man-made fibers. Finish may be soft or crisp. Weight is determined by the yarn construction, whether it is made with one, two, or three ply. May be recognized by its figure eight interlacing of warp and filling yarns.

Matelassé. The woven pattern stands out and gives a quilted, puckered, or blistered effect. A true matelassé is an adaptation of a double-cloth construction, made of either natural or man-made yarns. It may be described as two distinct fabrics woven together to produce the surface quilted effect when the total fabric is relaxed after the weaving. Fabrics that are sometimes called matelassé may be made by (1) interlacing crepe yarns with a straight yarn in both the warp and filling directions or in some cases in only the filling direction, (2) weaving with small dobby patterns on a box loom, (3) embossing to make the fabric look like a true matelassé.

Melton. A thick, heavily felted or fulled wool fabric (twill- or satin-weave) with a smooth, dull, napped surface. In the less expensive fabrics, the warp or lengthwise yarn may be cotton instead of wool. Used for overcoats, uniforms, and also for riding habits.

Milanese. See **Knit fabrics.**

Mohair. A hair fiber derived from the Angora goat. Mohair is often used in two entirely different types of fabric constructions:

(1) Mohair may be blended with wool and man-made fibers in a pile fabric construction for coating, drapery, and upholstery fabrics. It may be knitted with wool for sweaters.

(2) Mohair may be used with cotton, wool, or rayon and woven into shiny, stiff, wiry dress and suiting fabrics.

Monk's Cloth. Heavy, loosely woven basket-weave cotton fabric. May be plain-colored or have woven-in stripes or plaids. Used for draperies, slipcovers, hangings.

Mousseline de Soie. French term for silk muslin. A plain-weave, crisp, sheer fabric, more closely woven and stiffer than chiffon. Not so soft as voile. Yarns are highly twisted and sized before weaving.

Muslin. Term for a large group of plain-weave fabrics ranging from light to heavy weight. Usually made of cotton or blends of cotton and man-made fibers. Sizing may range from light to heavy. Fabrics may be bleached, unbleached, half bleached, solid colored, or printed. Used for dresses, household purposes. Wide muslin, used for sheets, is known as *sheeting*.

Net. Fabric made of thread knotted to form a mesh which may be fine and sheer or coarse and open. The meshes may be square, hexagonal, octagonal, or diamond shape. May be made on bobbinet lace machine and on knitting machine. Nets may be made from cotton, silk, or man-made fibers. Some well-known types of net are:

Bobbinet. Depending on the size of yarn, bobbinet may be very thin and transparent, or heavier and transparent like cotton bobbinet. These are made primarily in England and France.

Fish net. A coarse open-mesh fabric made by knotting meshes similar to a fisherman's knot.

Malines. A very, very fine open-diamond-shaped mesh net.

Tulle. A fine, small hexagonal mesh net fabric lighter in weight than bobbinet.

Ninon. A very thin, smooth, crisp plain-weave fabric made of silk or man-made fibers. Used for evening wear, lingerie.

Nonwoven Fabrics. See **Fabric Construction,** page 36.

Nun's Veiling. Very sheer, thin, soft, plain-weave wool fabric made with finely twisted yarns which give it a firm feel. Used for dresses, nuns' veiling.

Organdy. A term used to describe a crisp, sheer, transparent, lightweight cotton fabric, woven with tightly twisted, fine yarns. Durability of the crispness depends upon the type of finish. Organdy that is starched and calendered has a *nondurable crispness.* For *durable crispness,* fabric may be given a chemical finish by application of thermosetting resins that change the fiber itself and thereby produce a transparency and a silkiness as well as the longer-lasting crispness. Heberlein finish—an original Swiss process for producing permanent finish organdy—is considered to be extremely durable and satisfactory. See also **Silk Organdy.**

Organza. Similar to organdy, but more wiry and transparent. Made of silk or man-made fiber yarns. The yarns are highly twisted, ranging from 10 to 20 turns per inch.

Osnaburg. A rough, strong, plain-weave cotton fabric resembling crash. The yarns are uneven, producing a rough texture. Weight may vary from light to heavy. Used for sportswear, curtains, slipcovers, draperies.

Ottoman. Heaviest of the ribbed-weave fabrics. It has a large, heavy, rounded and pronounced cross-rib because of the three- to six-ply filling yarn of cotton, wool or cotton, wool, and man-made fibers. The single-ply yarn may be of silk or man-made fibers. Used for coats, dresses.

Oxford Cloth. A plain-weave or 2x2 basket-weave fabric made of cotton or man-made fiber yarns. Fabric may range from light to heavy weight; it is soft and has a silk-like luster. Used for shirting, sportswear, dresses.

Peau de Soie. Originally a silk fabric with an eight-shaft satin weave. Peau de soie is made in either single or double face construction; has a very smooth, silky, semi-dull appearance; and is much heavier than most satin constructions. Today, this fabric may be made of silk or of silk and man-made fiber yarns. Frequently used for bridal gowns.

Percale. Firm, smooth, plain-weave fabric that is starched and calendered and has little luster. Made of cotton or cotton and polyester blends. Used for curtains, bedspreads, dresses, shirts. *Percale sheets* are fine, smooth, and lustrous and have a high thread count.

Piqué. Term used to describe a class of ribbed-weave fabrics, medium to heavy weight, with varied surface textures formed by a raised rib or wale in the lengthwise direction of the fabric. These wales may vary in width and thickness. Piqué may be made by embossing a fabric to make it appear like a woven piqué fabric. These are some of the fabrics in this group.

    Bird's-eye piqué. The fabric may be woven or embossed with a characteristic small diamond-shaped design that has a dot in the center of each diamond shape.

    Pinwale piqué. Very fine cords running the lengthwise direction of the fabric.

    Waffle piqué. This fabric is woven with a raised cord to resemble a honeycomb or a waffle.

Polished Cotton. Plain-weave cotton fabrics characterized by a luster imparted by a finish.

Pongee. A thin, plain-weave silk fabric woven with irregular tussah or wild silk yarns in both warp and filling. The uneven yarns give it a broken crossbar effect. Characteristic color is ecru. Today pongee is simulated in man-made fibers. Used for blouses, dresses, shirts, curtains.

Poplin. Fine, closely woven fabric with slight horizontal ribs. It has heavier ribs, heavier yarns, and slightly lower thread count than broadcloth. Used for shirts, dresses, uniforms. Heavier weights may also be given a water-repellent finish for use as rainwear.

Ratiné. Loose, plain-weave fabric with nubby surface. Ratiné yarn gives the fabric a characteristic rough, spongy surface. May also be used in knitted constructions. A fabric for dresses, coats, suits.

Rep or Repp. Firmly woven, ribbed-weave fabric with a prominent rounded rib. May be of cotton, silk, or man-made fibers. The rib may run either in the warp or filling direction of the fabric.

Sailcloth. A very heavy, strong, plain-weave canvas fabric made of cotton, linen, jute, polyester, or nylon. There are many qualities and weights. Used for sails; also sportswear, slipcovers.

Sateen. Sateen is a cotton fabric of either a warp or filling satin weave. In the filling sateen, a filling yarn passes under one warp yarn and then floats over a number of warp yarns to again weave under one warp yarn, etc. The sheen is crosswise of the fabric. In a warp sateen, the warp passes under one filling yarn and then over a number of filling yarns, and again under one filling. A warp sateen is sometimes called satine. Some of these fabrics are mercerized and calendered to produce a high luster. Used for sportswear, dresses, draperies, comforter covers, bedspreads, slipcovers, linings.

Satin. Name of a weave, as well as of the fabric woven in this weave. Fabrics may be made of any fiber or combination of fibers and in different weights and qualities. Yarns are floated to the surface, in the satin weave, to give a lustrous face; thus, if the warp yarns are visible on the surface, the fabric is a warp-faced satin. There are many types of satins, and manufacturers use different trademark names to describe their particular satin fabric. Listed below are some of the most common types of satin fabrics:

Antique satin. A heavy fabric made to resemble silk satin of an earlier century. Used for home furnishing fabrics today.

Baronet satin. Very lustrous satin. Has a rayon face, cotton back. Usually dyed in brilliant shades.

Charmeuse. Medium-weight satin fabric with a high luster on the surface and a very dull back. Has a soft draping, clinging quality.

Ciré satin. Has a finish of wax applied under heat and pressure to give a very high luster and a degree of stiffness to the fabric.

Crepe-back satin. A soft, lustrous fabric that drapes well. Also called *satin-backed crepe* since it is reversible with the satin weave visible on one side and the crepe-twist filling yarns visible on the other side. Used for dresses, blouses, linings. Garments made of this fabric often use the contrasting side for trimming.

Panne satin. A highly lustrous satin with a stiff finish. Used for evening wear.

Slipper satin. Strong, heavy satin that is used chiefly for evening dress, wedding gowns, and other formal wear.

Scrim. A durable, open, plain-weave cotton or linen fabric. Made of coarse ply-yarns; may be mercerized. Used for curtains.

Seersucker. A true seersucker is a plain-weave fabric with permanent, woven-in, crinkled stripes running lengthwise in the fabric. Crinkled stripes are produced by slack warp tension in alternate groups of warp yarns. This distinguishes it from a plissé crepe produced by plissé printing. Fabric is made of cotton or man-made fibers. Used for sportswear, dresses, housecoats, bedspreads, curtains.

Serge. A twill-weave fabric with a pronounced right angle rib on both the right and wrong side. The lines run from lower left to upper right on the face of the fabric. There are many different weights of serge fabrics. For example, a "storm serge" is a coarse, wiry fabric, whereas a "French serge" is made of a very fine, soft yarn producing a fine twill. Silk serge is another name for surah. (See **Surah,** page 69.)

Shantung. Originally, shantung was a name for a hand-loomed, plain-weave fabric made in China. The fabric, made of wild silk, had an irregular surface. Today, shantung is a term that may be applied to a plain-weave fabric with heavier, irregular filling yarns. The fabric may be made of cotton, silk, or man-made fibers. There are certain terms used to describe various types of shantung.

Changeable shantungs. Sometimes called "antique shantung." The warp yarns are dyed one color, the filling yarns another. Sometimes the slub filling yarn is dyed several colors. This creates a changeable color on the surface of the fabric due to light reflection.

Douppioni shantung. The heaviest in weight of the shantung fabrics and the most expensive. The silk yarn used in douppioni shantung is made from cocoons that have nested in pairs; yarn is uneven and irregular.

Spun-silk shantung. Made of short lengths of silk fibers twisted together to form irregular slubs. Less expensive than douppioni shantung.

Sharkskin. There are two distinct types of sharkskin.

Sharkskin made of natural or man-made fibers. These may be described as sleek, hard-finished, crisp, yet pebbly-surfaced fabrics with a chalky luster. Filament yarns are twisted and woven tightly in either a plain- or basket-weave construction, depending upon the effect desired.

Wool sharkskin. This fabric is characterized by its twill weave. The yarns in both the warp and filling are alternated, white with a color, such as black, brown, or blue. The diagonal lines of the twill weave run from left to right; the colored yarns from right to left.

Silk Organdy. Lightweight silk fabric given a crisp finish either by natural gums or applied resin finishes. When this fabric is printed, it resembles mousseline de soie.

Straw Fabrics. Straw fabrics and designs are made from raffia and other plant fibers. Imitation-straw fabrics may be made from materials made to look like straw.

Monofilament rayon. Thick, flat, monofilament rayon fibers are twisted together to look like straw.

Cellophane. Cellophane strips are folded and twisted to look like straw.

Paper. High-strength paper is treated and cut into narrow strips and twisted to resemble straw.

Suede Cloth. Woven or knitted fabric of wool, rayon, or cotton finished to resemble suede leather. Generally heavier than duvetyn.

Surah. A semi-dull, soft, lightweight, twill-weave fabric which may be made of silk or man-made fibers. Has very definite diagonal lines (half right angle) and may be yarn-dyed to create plaids and checks or solid colors. May also be printed. The fabric is loom-finished. Sometimes called silk serge.

Taffeta. A fine, plain-weave fabric which has a heavier filling yarn than warp yarn, giving a fine-ribbed appearance. Actually, taffeta has approximately the same number of yarns in each direction, forming a firm, close weave with a characteristic dull luster and a stiffness that produces the rustle when the wearer of a taffeta garment moves.

Loom-finished taffetas. Most taffeta fabrics are loom-finished. The warp yarns are sized to give them the strength necessary to withstand the strains of weaving. Sizings are also used to impart the hand and rustle desired in the finished fabric. Sizings may be of two types: *Non-durable*, which may include the gelatins and gums that are water-soluble and may be affected by perspiration and moisture in wear and in cleaning; *Durable*, a class of sizings made up of different resin finishes that are not removed by drycleaning solvents.

Piece-dyed taffetas. Some taffetas are piece-dyed. They are soft rather than stiff as the loom-finished taffetas are because the sizing used in the weaving of the fabric is removed in a subsequent finishing operation.

Paper taffeta. Taffeta fabric given a lacquer finish for a high degree of stiffness and rustle.

Tapestry. A Jacquard-weave fabric woven with multicolored yarns. Made with two warp yarns and two or more filling yarns. Has a rough texture. Characterized by its distinctive tapestry pattern, large and pictorial. Used for draperies, wall hangings, upholstery.

Tarlatan. A lightweight, open, plain-weave fabric of cotton. It is transparent, stiffened, and sometimes glazed. Used for costumes, curtains, linings, stiffenings.

Tarnish-resistant Cloth. Soft, napped fabric treated with substances that protect silverware from tarnish.

Terry Cloth. Uncut pile-weave fabric of cotton, man-made fibers, or blends. Loops may be on one or both sides of the fabric. Designs may be woven in by the dobby- or Jacquard-weave method. Used for toweling, slipcovers, and wearing apparel such as bath or beach robes.

Ticking. This term covers a large group of cotton and linen fabrics made of a twill, herringbone twill, satin, or Jacquard weave. May be used as upholstery, and mattress and pillow covers.

Tricot. See **Knit Fabrics.**

Tropical Worsted or Summer Suiting. Lightweight suiting widely used for men's summer business suits and women's suits. Plain weave with hard-twisted yarns is used to give a clear finish. Made of all one fiber or blends of fibers.

Tweed. Name is derived from the River Tweed in Scotland where these fabrics were first woven. Today the name refers to a wide range of light- to heavyweight, rough-textured, sturdy fabrics which are characterized by their mixed-color effect. May be made of plain, twill, or herringbone weave of practically any fiber or mixture of fibers. May be monocolored (different shades of the same color), checked, plaid, striped, patterned. Certain names are famous among tweeds.

Harris tweed. Trademark name for a fabric made by hand in the Outer Hebrides off the

Tweed (Continued)

coast of Scotland. The dye in the yarns is cooked over peat, the smell of which often remains in the fabric and may become noticeable when the fabric becomes damp.

Donegal tweed. This is a thick fabric made of colorful slubs like the original homespun tweeds. They are handwoven in Donegal County, Ireland.

Velcro® brand hook and loop fasteners. Trademark name (American Velcro, Inc.) for a fastener consisting of two woven nylon strips which, when pressed together, adhere to each other. One strip looks and feels like velvet; the other is covered with tiny nylon hooks that mesh with the velvet side to form a fastening which can be opened by pulling either strip back. Typical uses are in wearing apparel, slipcovers.

Velour (also **Velours**). The terms velour and plush are used interchangeably for pile velour construction. Velour also includes a variety of woolen fabrics characterized by a short, soft, thick pile, with either a twill or satin background and a velour finish. Velour fabrics may be made of cotton, wool, silk, mohair, or man-made fibers. These fabrics may be distinguished from duvetyn because they have a thicker and longer nap, and the base weave is not concealed as in duvetyn fabrics.

Velvet. The many different types of velvet are all made of a pile construction. The pile may be cut, uncut, or cut and uncut. Velvets may be made of silk, wool, mohair, or man-made fibers. Background may be a plain, twill, or satin weave. Velvet and pile constructions are classed as V-type or W-type. In the V-type, the pile goes under only one warp yarn; in the W-type, the pile goes under and over two warp yarns. Certain terms used to describe certain definite types of velvet are:

Chiffon velvet. A lightweight, soft velvet with a short, thick pile. This type of velvet may be made from silk or the man-made fibers.

Cotton-backed velvet. Cotton background weave; silk or man-made fibers used in the pile.

Lyons velvet. A heavy, crisp, closely woven, stiff fabric with an erect, short, thick pile. It may have a cotton or silk back with a silk or man-made fiber pile.

Silk velvet. Silk background weave; silk pile.

Transparent velvet. A very lightweight, soft velvet that can be seen through when held to the light.

Velvet fabrics may be treated to give them an appearance different from the regular-type velvets. These specially treated fabrics may be described as follows:

Crushed velvet. Fabric is placed between rollers, and heat, moisture, and pressure are applied. The pile is not pressed in one direction, like that of panne velvet; hence, there is a variation of reflection of the pile, creating a mixed effect, dull with bright.

Embossed velvet. May also be called "sculptured velvet." In making this fabric, the design is engraved on a metal roll. The velvet fabric, under conditions of steam, heat, and pressure, is passed under the roll. The raised areas on the roll flatten the background areas and produce a shiny background surface that contrasts with the design.

Faconné velvet. This is sometimes called brocaded velvet. The fabric is woven like other velvets, then chemicals are applied in the desired pattern to the back of the fabric. This treatment carbonizes the pile when it is heated and leaves the untreated pile to form the pattern. The background weave that is unaffected by the chemical treatment is readily visible on the right side of the fabric.

Moiréed velvet. Fabric is passed through rollers engraved with a design. In the presence of heat, pressure, and moisture, the design is transferred to the fabric. Some of these fabrics are given a water-repellent finish.

Panne velvet. Has a rich-looking, satiny appearance because the pile is pressed down in one direction as the fabric passes over rollers in the presence of steam and pressure.

Velvet with metallic yarns. Metallic yarns are woven into the velvet construction to create beautiful and unusual designs.

Velveteen. Classed as a filling pile construction because two sets of filling yarns are used to one warp yarn. One filling yarn is woven with the warp yarn to form the ground weave (plain or twill). The other filling yarn is woven into the warp at intervals and then floats over a number of warp yarns. When fabric is woven, the floating filling yarns are cut and brushed to form the short, closely set pile. The pile is not as erect as that of velvet. It slopes slightly, thus making the fabric surface lustrous.

Voile. Sheer, transparent, soft, lightweight, plain-weave fabric made of highly twisted, combed yarns. May be made of wool, cotton, silk, or a man-made fiber. Used for blouses, dresses, curtains, bedspreads.

Waffle Cloth. See **Honeycomb.**

Whipcord. Twill-weave fabric made of wool, cotton, or man-made fibers, or blends of a man-made fiber with a natural fiber. The diagonal lines of the weave are very steep and usually run from left to right. In some fabrics, the back or underside of the fabric is napped slightly. The fabric may be in a solid color, or colored fibers may be mixed with white fibers resulting in a salt-and-pepper effect. Used for dresses, suits, topcoats, many types of uniforms.

Zibeline. Made of wool, cotton, camel's hair, mohair, or man-made fibers. Fabric has a basic satin weave hidden by a characteristic long, sleek nap that has been brushed, steamed, and pressed in one direction.

Maintenance of Fabrics

The method of cleaning a fabric may be determined by the kind of soil or the fabric itself. However, the fundamental cleaning process for all textiles involves the immersion and agitation of each item in a solvent.

Soiling and staining of fabrics are caused by waterborne or oil-borne substances; or dry substances which are rubbed into a fabric or which settle from the air. *Greasy or oil-borne substances* are removed by dissolving in drycleaning organic solvents or by emulsifying them in a detergent and water solution. *Waterborne substances* are removed by water. *Dry substances* are removed by shaking or brushing; or during laundering or drycleaning, by lubrication or the removal of oil which binds the soil to the fabric.

Textile items may be classified by the type of cleansing to which they can be subjected. For example, in a standard of the American National Standards Institute, L22, each of the items in the standard is classified in one of four cleansing categories:

Washable at 160°F, with bleach
Washable at 160°F, no bleach
Washable at 120°F, no bleach
Drycleanable only

Many fabrics may be both drycleaned and laundered without any injurious effect. Certain fabrics, because of finish or fabric construction, may not be washed without undesirable alteration of the fabric. Ordinarily these fabrics can be drycleaned successfully. A few other fabrics which contain a component such as a bonding agent or a plasticizer that is adversely affected or is soluble in drycleaning solvent, cannot be drycleaned satisfactorily. Usually items made of these fabrics can be washed. Some fabrics cannot be drycleaned without fading because there are a few dyes that are soluble in drycleaning solvents. Fabrics that can be washed are not all equally washable. Occasionally there is a fabric that cannot be drycleaned or laundered so that the end product is acceptable.

Care instructions must be attached to essentially all apparel sold, whether imported or domestic. Care labeling laws also include fabrics sold by the yard. (See page 97.)

Professional Cleaning

When garments or household items are received for professional cleaning, they are marked for identification and inspected. Rips, tears, or unusual stains are noted, as well as fabrics or garment constructions that require special handling. Breakable articles such as buckles, buttons, and ornaments are removed and sent to the sewing department for replacement later on the cleaned and finished garment.

The garments are then sorted according to types and classified. Pockets, cuffs, and seams are brushed to remove loose soil and lint. This reduces the risk of transfer of lint to other garments. Pockets are searched for such items as ball-point pens, lipsticks, and knives, which are great hazards to other garments during cleaning.

Any heavy soil, spots, or stains that have water as an integral part must be removed by either a prespotting or prebrushing treatment, or spotting after cleaning. Light watersoluble soil is removed by the controlled relative humidity of the cleaning solvent. Some stains such as grass stains, gutter-splash, and paint stains, are set more tenaciously if they are not removed before cleaning. Methods of professional cleaning include the following:

Drycleaning

The drycleaning of modern-day fabrics and intricate garment design has become quite complicated. However, the fundamental process for all items involves the immersion and agitation of the garment in solvent.

Solvents, Soaps, and Detergents. There are two general classifications of drycleaning solvent: *Petroleum* and *Synthetic (perchlorethylene, trichlorotrifluoroethane)*. Most drycleaning in this country is done in perchlorethylene.

The commercial soaps and detergents are different from those used at home, but they perform the same function when used with drycleaning solvents in helping to carry loose soil. used with drycleaning solvents, that is, they help carry loose soil.

Drycleaning solvents are purified by two basic means: (1) *Continuous filtration* removes solids such as dust and lint by rapid flow of solvent from the washer through a filter medium. Various filter aids such as diatomaceous earth, activated carbon, and absorbent powders are used to keep the solvent in good condition.

(2) *Distillation* removes soluble soil such as body oils, makeup, and food from the solvent. Distillation is also used to provide a continuous supply of fresh, clean solvent.

Specialized Equipment. The washing cylinder of a drycleaning machine is built to supply the mechanical action necessary to remove soil from the fabrics. Ribs may be built inside the cylinder to aid in picking the garments up and then dropping them, and the cylinder is perforated to allow the solvent to flow through.

Spotting and Deodorizing. After cleaning and rinsing of items, solvent is removed from the garments by extraction—the removal of solvent from the garments by centrifugal force—and in a tumbler or cabinet in which a current of warm, fresh air is circulated through the garments.

If a garment is not a specialty item, it goes through these processes with a number of other garments. In the following processes, it is handled individually, going next to the spotting department for inspection and removal of any spots and stains. The spotter is required to have a knowledge of textile fibers, fabric construction, dyestuffs, and chemicals, as well as special skills and techniques.

The main problem in spot and stain removal is to remove stains safely. However, all stains cannot be removed safely. A competent drycleaner can detect the margin of safety and will not risk injury to the fabric.

Finishing. When garments are cleaned and possible spots removed, they are sent to the proper finishing department. The term "finishing" is used rather than "pressing," because often no mechanical pressure is used. Only steam and air are applied. Pressure is not applied in the same manner as in home pressing. Presses have been built to accommodate most fabrics, and equipment designed for various sizes and shapes of garments. Some garments lend themselves readily to steam-air finishing so that an entire garment may be finished on a garment form that is inflated with air.

Fabrics containing natural fibers are softened by steam. Thermoplastic fabrics are softened by heat transfer. Steam is the source of heat. After the fabric is softened, the garment is cooled to its original shape. A portion of the garment such as the lining may be touched up by hand pressing. Some cleaners now use conditioning cabinets to remove wrinkles from certain garment types and then finish the pressing with hand touch-up.

A puff iron is used to finish intricate folds or frills. Puff irons consist of perforated metal forms, padded and covered, and made into various sizes and shapes. A press with a smooth polished head surface is used for finishing such smooth lustrous fabrics as satins and taffetas; whereas a press with a perforated head surface is used for such dull finished fabrics as crepes. Depending on the garment, a conventional hand and steam iron may also be used in finishing.

After the garment is finished, buttons, ornaments, and trimming that were removed prior to drycleaning are replaced. Minor rips, tears, and broken seams and hem lines are repaired, and the garment is given a final inspection.

Wetcleaning

When garments are so badly soiled that drycleaning does not remove all the soil, they must be further cleaned by a process known as wetcleaning. Garments that may need bleaching, or garments that are so stained that they require the digestive action of enzymes, can be cleaned by wet processing.

Wetcleaning is not washing. However, it is removal of soil with water. Wetcleaning differs from washing in that (1) garments are drycleaned first to remove solvent-soluble soil; (2) garments are measured and, when necessary, restored to original size after wetcleaning; (3) dyes are tested to determine proper treatment; (4) garments are given the least possible mechanical action whether hand-brushed or machine-processed (mechanical action may or may not be required depending upon type of soil to be removed); (5) garments are treated according to fabric construction in extracting, drying, sizing, and other handling processes.

Quick drying is essential in wetcleaning. To accomplish this, a wind-whip and drying cabinet is used. The unit is heated to hasten drying and thus helps to eliminate possibility of bleeding and streaking of the dye.

Coin-Operated Drycleaning

Since the innovation of the coin-operated drycleaning machine, "do-it-yourself" drycleaning has become popular.

The coin-operated drycleaning machine resembles a combination washer-dryer in appearance and in the way it tumbles items in a cylinder. A special safe nonflammable solvent (perchlorethylene or fluorocarbon) is used. For best results the machines should not be overloaded, and some sorting is advisable to separate dark from light and bulky from sheer items. The customer needs to take the same preparatory steps that the drycleaner does—remove trimming that will not dryclean, turn pockets inside out and brush them, close zippers, turn down cuffs, brush spots caused by food or sugary substances, place items that may snag in nylon net or mesh bags.

The machine goes through a set pattern of cycles, usually requiring a time cycle of 45 to 60 minutes for cleaning and drying. When the machine stops the clothes should be removed and put on hangers immediately.

Coin-operated drycleaning appeals to customers because it is economical and convenient. Although professional spot cleaning and pressing may be needed for some items, coin-operated drycleaning is particularly popular for items that do not require much finishing or for items, such as blankets, that might not be sent to a professional cleaner.

Commercial Laundering

The first steps in handling items to be laundered commercially are identifying and classifying. During classification, the fabrics are separated into groups such as white, light color, dark color, white shirts, wool, man-made, and heavily soiled white. Up to 12 classifications may be used depending on such things as color, fiber content, and degree of soil.

After identification and classification, the fabrics are washed. The method used to wash a particular article is determined by its classification. Laundries differ in their procedures but the washing formula in the accompanying table is an example of those used in commercial laundries.

Only soft waters are used since hard water wastes supplies and forms deposits on washers and in water lines. In most cases, a laundryman will use soap rather than a detergent because he generally has a water softener.

Periodically, samples of water from each operation are taken to determine whether the concentrations of alkali, soap, bleach, and sour are within prescribed limits.

If white clothes are being washed at the usual 140° to 160°F, a high-titre soap will be used because it gives the best suds and cleansing action at these temperatures. For washing wools at 90°F, a low-titre soap is used because this gives the best suds and cleansing action at low temperature.

Laundry Procedures and Equipment. For wool articles a special machine is used. It gently rolls the articles through heavy suds at a very low rate of speed. A neutral soap or detergent is used. No alkali is added to this formula to prevent a deteriorating effect upon the wool. Three to five rinses are generally used in order to remove all of the soap. If this is not done, an off-color discoloration in the fabric may result. The souring operation that follows acts as a final rinse. On wool, the souring operation may act as a mothproofing treatment if sufficient amounts of sour are used.

Because silk is chemically similar to wool, it is washed in the same manner. A neutral soap or detergent is used. Chlorine-type bleaches are never used because they would yellow and damage the silk. Also, highly alkaline material would damage the silk. Soiled curtains and draperies are washed gently like wools, because they may have been weakened by light.

Light-colored fabrics of all fibers are washed

WASHING FORMULA FOR BLEACHABLE WHITE ARTICLES

Operation	Supplies	Temperature	Time
Suds	Soap or detergent and alkali	125°F	5-10 min.
Suds	Soap or detergent and alkali	145°F	5-10 min.
Suds	Soap or detergent and alkali	160°F	5-10 min.
Bleach[1]	2 quarts 1 percent bleach per 100 pounds dry clothes put in washer	160°F	5 min.
Rinse	Nothing added	160°F	3-5 min.
Rinse	Nothing added	140°F	3-5 min.
Rinse	Nothing added	120°F	3-5 min.
Rinse	Nothing added	100°F	3-5 min.
Sour[2]	Sour to pH of approximately 5	100°F	5 min.
Bluing	Bluing material	Cold	5 min.

[1] A number of types of bleaches are used. Sodium hypochlorite is commonly used. It will have a concentration no greater than 1 percent available chlorine when it is added to the wash wheel. This 1 percent available chlorine is between one-fifth and one-sixth the amount of available chlorine in most home laundry bleaches. Some calcium hypochlorite dry bleaches are also used. The calcium hypochlorite is combined with phosphates to prevent the calcium from precipitating soap. In other cases, organic-type chlorine bleaches are used.

[2] The souring operation is similar to adding vinegar or lemon juice to the rinse water when shampooing the hair. It neutralizes the alkalinity in the water. It also helps to remove iron stains and helps to kill bacteria.

at temperatures between 100° to 120°F. Because dark colors have a greater tendency to bleed than have light colors, the dark colors are washed at lower temperatures, 90° to 100°F.

In commercial laundering only white articles are bleached. If stain removal is necessary on colored items, they receive a special treatment.

After articles are washed, they are taken out of the washers and placed in extractors which spin the clothes to remove excess water. Over-extraction is avoided, especially for articles containing man-made fibers in order to avoid setting permanent wrinkles in the fabrics. Many laundries used washer-extractor combinations so that apparel and household linens can be washed and extracted without transfer to another unit.

After extraction, the articles are sorted and sent to different areas of the laundry for proper finishing or drying. Generally, customers may choose among a variety of finishes offered by the laundry. They may have everything tumble-dried, only the flat pieces (sheets, tablecloths, and pillowcases) pressed and the rest of the bundle tumble-dried, or everything pressed, in which case, all wearing apparel would be finished and returned to the customer ready to wear or use.

Flat pieces are finished or pressed on what is called a flatwork ironer. Fabrics pass between a smooth, heated metal surface and large cloth-covered rolls. This dries the fabric, removes wrinkles, and applies a sheen to the surface.

One question often posed about laundries is: How do they get everything to feel starched? This so-called starch is merely a temporary stiffness which leaves as soon as the fabric flexes. It is the result of the pressing operation on the flatwork ironer. In home ironing, rubbing the iron back and forth across the fabric flexes the fibers enough so that they become soft immediately. Since the laundry-pressed garment is not flexed, it feels starched until it is used. Most laundries follow the customer's wishes about putting starch in garments.

Heated puff irons, small presses, handkerchief presses, sock forms, large flat presses for curtains, special curtain stretchers, and blanket carders and shapers are all used to finish various types of articles. Special equipment has been designed to press a shirt in a minute.

After the finishing process, the articles are brought to one location for packaging.

Home Laundering

Washing Procedures and Home-Use Products

Modern washers are nearly capable of performing laundering miracles, but for best results clothes should be prepared for the washer, and suitable laundry products and methods should be used.

These are good rules to follow before washing is started:

• Mend garments with rips, tears, or holes; close snaps and zippers; and empty pockets.

• Sort clothes into washer loads, putting together those that require the same water temperature, length of washing time, and type of washing products.

• If the washer features multiple speeds, consider also the proper speed for the various items when separating garments.

• In general, separate white clothes into one group, colored ones into another group; also separate heavily soiled garments from delicate fabrics. Frail or delicate items may be placed in a mesh bag or pillowcase.

• Check garments for stains. Some stains should be treated separately before garments are washed. A detergent presoak is effective on many stains and soils, particularly if the detergent is an enzyme product. Use warm rather than hot water for presoaking. Hot water may set some stains.

• If a presoak is not used, pretreat heavily soiled areas by applying soap or detergent directly to the wet garment and by rubbing or brushing the product into the soiled places.

• Test new colored items for colorfastness on a concealed part of the garment in a solution of detergent and/or other laundry products with the water at the temperature likely to be used for general laundering. If a garment is to be pre-treated with concentrated detergent, test this too on a seam or other hidden part.

Because each make of washer has its own unique washing system and because some models of washers provide more choices of cycles than others, it is best to follow the washer manufacturer's directions for care of each type of clothes load. The regular cycle is designed for bed, bath, and table linens and sturdily constructed garments. Delicate cycles provide reduced washing time and/or slower washing action to protect more fragile items. Durable-press or wash-and-wear cycles provide special cooling rinses and slow spin speed to minimize wrinkling.

All types of garments can be handled in wringer washers too, but more attention and effort are required. A few general rules for *wringer washers* are:

• Allow 10 to 15 minutes for regular family loads.

• Reduce wash time to four to six minutes for delicate things.

• To minimize wrinkling, wash durable-press garments in warm water unless they are heavily soiled and require hot water for maximum cleaning. Use cold water for rinsing. Do not wring garments when they are warm. After cold rinses some items may be suitable to put through the wringer with light pressure setting.

Water Conditioners. Soft water produces the best results in laundering. Hard water contains hardness minerals, primarily calcium and magnesium. In theory, soft water does not. But water is rarely totally soft because seldom can all of the hardness minerals be removed, precipitated, or locked up.

For practical purposes, water hardness is generally measured in terms of grains per gallon (gpg). The local water authority can usually provide specific water hardness information. The following chart classifies the degree of hardness.

Soft	Medium Hard	Hard	Very Hard
Up to 3 grains per gallon	4 to 9 grains per gallon	10 to 15 grains per gallon	Over 15 grains per gallon

To soften water is to remove, precipitate, or

sequester (lock up) the hardness minerals. There are two ways of softening water. One is to install a water-softening appliance. By a process of ion exchange, all water flowing through this appliance is softened before it flows from the faucet. The other means of softening water is through the use of packaged softeners. These products are added to the water in sink or washer.

Packaged water softeners may be classified as either *precipitating type* or *non-precipitating type* (water conditioners).

When a precipitating softener is added to water, it combines with the hardness mineral ions and forms a precipitate (a visible insoluble solid). This precipitate makes the water appear cloudy and can attach itself to fabrics in the wash.

The non-precipitating water conditioner softens by "sequestering" the hardness minerals. The conditioner surrounds and locks up the hardness minerals in water and soil, but without forming visible solid particles or precipitates. The water does not cloud.

When a soap product is used in hard water, a water softening product should be added to both the wash and rinse water. With a detergent, however, there is no need to use a water softener unless the water is very hard. If the water is very hard or if there is iron present in the water, a non-precipitating type of water conditioner will be helpful.

The following are some of the water softening compounds and water conditioners available. Italics indicate brand names with manufacturers in parentheses. (See Appendix for full names and addresses of manufacturers.)

Precipitating. *Climalene* (Climalene Company); *Mel-O* (Boyle-Midway); *Oakite* (Oakite Products); *Perfex* (Tidy House); sal soda and washing soda (generic names).

Non-precipitating. *Calgon* (Calgon Corporation); *Spring Rain* (Tidy House).

Water Temperature. Hot water (at least 140°F) has been found to be the most efficient in soil removal. However, there are times when warm water (about 100°F) is needed to preserve color or finish, reduce shrinkage, or minimize wrinkling of easy care fabrics. For cold-water washing, a number of especially formu-

lated detergents are available. Cold water can be used for all rinsing and may be particularly helpful in minimizing wrinkling of man-made fiber fabrics and blends.

Detergents and Soaps. The term *detergent* is defined by the Association of Home Appliance Manufacturers as "a laundry product designed to remove, emulsify, dissolve, and suspend soil in a washing solution. Home laundry usage currently limits meaning to synthetic, non-soap compounds which are distinguished from soap principally by not forming lime soap in hard water. *Synthetic detergent* and *detergent* are used interchangeably. Technically, soaps are detergents, but in current popular usage are not referred to as such." [1]

Soaps and detergents may be classified according to use. *Mild soaps and detergents* are generally used for fine fabrics and for dishwashing. *All-purpose (heavy-duty or laundry) soaps and detergents* can be used for washing heavily soiled garments as well as fine fabrics. These products are commonly used in washing machines.

Today all-purpose (heavy-duty or laundry) soaps are available only in limited markets. No single brand is sold nationally. Family laundry is done almost exclusively with all-purpose detergents.

The laundry detergents can be further classified by sudsing characteristics; *high (normal) sudsers, intermediate sudsers,* and *low sudsers.* The high and intermediate sudsers can be used in all top-loading washers, whether the machine is of the automatic or wringer variety. The low sudsers can be used in all washers, but offer a special advantage in front loading, tumbler-type automatic washers where an excessive amount of suds can interfere with the washing action. Since detergent products may vary in density, it is important to follow package directions for the amount to be used. All package recommendations for machine use are based on moderate soil in an average amount of water (about 16 gallons in a top-loading washer; 8 gallons in a front loader) of average hardness (i.e., 5 to 7 grains per

---

[1] Home Laundering Terms, American Home Laundry Manufacturers' Association (now the Association of Home Appliance Manufacturers), Chicago, Illinois, revised 1965.

Home Laundering (Continued)

gallon). Large loads of clothes, very dirty clothes, or hard water will require more product.

While each detergent product has its own unique formula, there are certain basic types of ingredients common to all these products. These ingredients are:

Surface active agents (surfactants) improve the wetting ability of water and loosen, make soluble, and/or suspend soil. The surfactants used in all laundry products are biodegradable.

Builders (primarily complex phosphates) sequester hardness minerals, disperse and suspend dirt, maintain desirable alkalinity, and aid surfactant efficiency. In some parts of the country, phosphate-built detergents are banned to reduce eutrophication of surface water in lakes and slow streams. Detergents and other builders (mainly carbonates) have been substituted. These products, however, clean less efficiently than do phosphate-built detergents. Carbonates, furthermore, unless used in soft water, may stiffen fabrics or cause problems such as skin rashes or washer troubles while improvement in the quality of surface water remains only a hope.

Suds control agents establish and control desired sudsing characteristics.

Silicates impart crispness to free flowing granules and provide a reserve of alkalinity that helps protect metal washer parts.

Soil redeposition inhibitors (usually carboxymethyl cellulose) aid in keeping soil, once it has been removed, from redepositing on fabrics during the balance of the washing process.

Fluorescent whitening agents (essentially colorless fluorescent dyes) attach to the fabric and convert invisible ultraviolet energy and reradiate it in the form of visible light which results in a whiter, brighter-appearing fabric.

Perfume provides a pleasant product impression, helps cover odor from soiled clothes during washing, and leaves a clean fragrance on the clothes after washing.

In addition to the ingredients common to all detergents, one or more of the following optional ingredients may be incorporated into a laundry product:

Oxygen bleach (usually sodium perborate) aids in removal of some soils and stains. This is most effective under conditions of high temperature or prolonged soaking.

Borax imparts sweetness and freshness to clothes and aids in removal of some soils.

Bacteriostats inhibit the growth of some bacteria on washed fabrics.

Bluings leave a slight blue tint on fabrics and thus tend to counteract yellowing.

Colorants (other than bluing) impart individuality to a product or dramatize special additives that contribute to product performance.

Enzymes reduce complex soils, especially proteins, to simpler forms that can be more easily removed by the other detergent ingredients and the washing action. Enzymes are particularly effective on blood stains, grass stains, body soil, egg, milk, gravy, and other protein-food stains. However, severe stains may call for more than the usual soak or washing time; hence the use of enzyme action in pre-soak products and the increased emphasis on soaking as an accepted practice in home laundering. The enzymes in both types of products will not affect fibers, fabric finishes, or dyestuffs adversely.

The use of enzymes in laundry products is a relatively recent development made possible by the discovery of enzymes that will remain active in the ranges of alkilinity and temperatures encountered in home laundering.

Bleaches. Bleaching is a long standing and respected custom which has a rightful place in the laundry of today. Bleach very ably complements detergent performance by helping to remove certain types of soil. In addition, bleach whitens fabrics, removes many stains, and disinfects and deodorizes.

There are three types of bleach readily available to the homemaker.

Liquid chlorine-type bleaches. These are the most widely used, most effective, and least expensive of the bleaching products. Most of the liquid bleach produced for household use contains, as its active ingredient, sodium hypochlorite. These bleaches may be used on white and colorfast cottons and linens and on all man-made fiber fabrics except some spandex fibers. Most of the finishes used on durable-press or wash-and-wear fabrics are also bleachable. A few fabric finishes may be chlorine retentive. Chlorine-type bleaching should not be used on such fabrics. Hang tags may carry the necessary precautions.

The liquid chlorine bleaches must be diluted before they are allowed to come in contact with the clothes. A bleach dispenser on an automatic washer will do this automatically, and many dispensers will delay the addition of the bleach to the wash water. Delaying the addition of the bleach for four to six minutes is ideal because chlorine bleach will reduce the effectiveness of the fluorescent fabric whiteners in the detergent product unless the whiteners have had a chance to become affixed to the fabrics; also, chlorine bleach will inactivate the enzymes in detergents which contain them. The few minutes of delay will permit the fabric whiteners, enzymes, and bleach all to do their work effectively. If the addition of bleach is delayed manually by the user, the recommended amount of bleach should be diluted with at least a quart of water before it is added to the wash load.

Caution: Always follow package directions for use. *Do not use* liquid chlorine-type bleaches on silks, woolens, or blends containing these fibers.

Dry chlorine bleaches. These are heavy-duty dry bleaches (mostly chlorinated triazine-triones). Once these bleaches are dissolved in water, they act in somewhat the same manner as liquid chlorine-type bleaches. Like the liquids, dry chlorine bleaches are safe for white and colorfast cottons, linens, rayons, and other man-made fibers except spandex. Care should be taken not to pour dry chlorine bleach directly onto colored clothes.

Caution: Follow package directions for use. *Do not use* on silks, woolens, or blends containing these fibers or on chlorine retentive resin finished fabrics.

Dry oxygen bleaches. These are "light duty" bleaches, rather mild in action. In this category are sodium perborate and other peroxy compounds, including potassium monopersulfate. They work best on fresh stains and lightly soiled fabrics. They can be used safely on all fibers— natural and man-made. Oxygen bleaches are safe for most colors. Since a few colors may be sensitive to these bleaches, these products should not be poured directly onto colored clothes. Bleach should be in solution before colored clothes are added.

As has been indicated, to get the best results

from any bleach, it is essential to read and follow package label directions carefully.

When there is doubt about whether or not to use bleach on a garment or other item, this *bleach test* is generally a safe precaution:

Snip a small sample of fabric from a seam allowance, facing, or hem. Soak about five minutes in the same strength solution to be used in bleaching.

If colors are not colorfast but some fading or color change can be tolerated, the item may be laundered separately in cool water with bleach. To keep colors uniform, bleach entire item. *Do not spot bleach.*

Following are some bleaches for home laundry use. Italics indicate brand names with the manufacturer in parentheses. (See Appendix for full names and addresses.)

(1) **Chlorine, liquid.** *Clorox* (Clorox); *Fleecy White* (Purex); *Linco* (Linco); *Purex Super Bleach* (Purex); *Roman* (Roman Cleanser Company).

(2) **Chlorine, dry** (also referred to as powdered or granular). *Action* (Colgate-Palmolive); *Hilex* (Hilex); *Linco* (Linco).

(3) **Peroxygen, liquid.** Hydrogen peroxide (generic name).

(4) **Peroxygen, dry.** *All-Fabric Beads-O'-Bleach* (Purex); *Daybrite* (Boyle-Midway); *Dexol* (Tidy House); *Lestare* (Standard Household Products); *Miracle White* (Beatrice Foods); *Snowy* (Gold Seal); *Vano* (Chemicals, Inc.; see Babbitt).

Disinfectants. Disinfectants used in the laundry must kill bacteria without leaving any residue which might be harmful to the skin, and without changing the color or other properties of the fabric. They are not major washday ingredients, since it is generally agreed that under normal conditions, laundering with hot water and soap or detergent followed by dryer-drying or air-drying in sunshine out-of-doors produces a sanitary wash. However, if there is illness in the family, research indicates that the use of a disinfectant during laundering can help prevent possible spread of disease-causing bacteria especially when items are laundered in communal washing facilities.

Home Laundering (Continued)

Among the most effective disinfectants are liquid chlorine bleach and pine oil products—available in most groceries—and quaternary compounds and phenolic compounds usually available in drug or household supply stores. To be effective they must *all* be used according to directions. These, too, must be kept out of the hands of children.

Here are some examples of disinfectants (other than chlorine bleaches). Italics indicate brand names with manufacturers in parentheses. (See Appendix for full names and addresses of manufacturers.)

Quaternary. *Co-Op Sanitizer* (Greenbelt Consumer Services); *Roccal* (Sterwin Chemicals)

Phenolic. *Pine-Sol* (American Cyanamid)

Pine Oil. *Fyne-Pyne* (H. A. Cole); *King Pine* (Johnson Chemical Co.)

Fabric Softeners. Fabric softeners are among the most popular laundry ingredients though they have only been available since the mid-fifties. Often referred to as fabric conditioners, they lubricate the individual fibers with an oil-like film, doing much more than just softening. Not only do they make diapers, terrys, corduroys, sweaters, and other high-napped fabrics feel softer and fluffier, they also reduce wrinkling, prevent clinging due to static electricity—especially in nylon and other synthetic fibers—and make ironing easier, sometimes unnecessary. When fabric softener is used, many wash-and-wear garments which ordinarily would require some touch-up ironing become truly wash-and-wear with no ironing needed. Softener also improves the appearance and hand or feel of durable press.

Today's fabric softeners may or may not contain bluing, brighteners, and bacteriostats to counteract yellowing and to help sanitize. Available in both liquid and powdered form, some are even packaged in individual pre-measured packets.

All fabric softeners must be added in the final rinse because, in general, they are not compatible with soaps, detergents, and other laundry aids. Some washers have a dispenser that automatically injects fabric softener at the right time in the rinse cycle.

Because some fabric softeners are more concentrated than others, it is especially important to follow the directions for recommended amounts. Too little is ineffective and too much can reduce moisture absorption and thereby make some fabrics almost waterproof. Towels, for example, can lose some of their drying ability. Since the effects of softeners are cumulative, it is suggested that after every few washes, their use be skipped for a wash. Similarly, if a build-up should occur from over-use, fabric softener should be omitted for a wash or two until the excess is washed out.

Following are some fabric softeners and antistatic agents. Italics indicate brand name with manufacturer in parentheses. (See Appendix for full names and addresses.)

Downy (Procter & Gamble); *Final Touch* (Lever Brothers); *King Fluff* (Mangels, Herold); *Nu-Soft* (Best Foods); *Right* (du Pont); *Sta-Puf* (A. E. Staley).

Starches. In the United States, vegetable starches used for laundry applications are derived largely from corn. Starching of fabrics is done for several reasons: (1) to replace the finish which may have been lost through repeated washings; (2) to impart body and crispness to the fabric; (3) to obtain a stiff, neat appearance; (4) to help keep a garment clean for a longer time by holding down tiny surface fibers which catch dust; and (5) to facilitate soil removal since soil attaches to the starch rather than to the fabric and is removed with starch during washing.

The major emphasis in the starching of today's modern fabrics must be placed on aerosol starches and fabric finishes. They provide a neat but softer finish. In addition to the traditional reasons for using starches; aerosols offer convenience, simplicity of operation, cleanliness, a consistent dispersion, and are free from contamination and deterioration. These attributes explain the rising popularity of aerosols over older methods of applying starch which required preparation before the starch could be used and therefore took more time and effort.

Recent additions to aerosol sizings are the fabric finishes. Aerosol fabric finishes generally provide less stiffness and impart a more flexible finish to fabrics. They are especially suited to the multitude of synthetic fabrics and fiber blends currently in use.

Liquid and dry starches continue to find use in larger scale dipping and washer sizing applications. Liquid starches are precooked, easy to dilute, and ready to use. Dry starches are the most economical, but must be cooked or mixed with hot water prior to use. In a separate dry starch category are cold water soluble starches, which may simply be mixed with cool water before use.

Following is a partial list of the laundry starches and fabric finishes available on the market today. Italics indicate brand names with manufacturer in parentheses. (See Appendix for complete names and addresses).

Spray starches. *Easy-On* (Boyle-Midway, Inc.); *Faultless* (Faultless Starch Co.); *Niagara* (Best Foods Division, CPC International); *Pruf* (Colgate-Palmolive); *Sta-Flo* (A. E. Staley).

Spray fabric finishes (or sizings). *Babo 4-in-1* (B. T. Babbitt, Inc.); *Faultless* (Faultless Starch Co.); *Magic Finish* (Armour-Dial); *Niagara* (Best Foods Division, CPC International); *Sta-Flo* (A. E. Staley).

Liquid starches. *Linit* (Best Foods Division, CPC International); *Sta-Flo* (A. E. Staley).

Dry starches. *Argo Gloss* (Best Foods Division, CPC International); *Faultless* (Faultless Starch Co.); *Linit* (Best Foods Division, CPC International); *Niagara Instant* (Best Foods Division, CPC International).

Drying

Drying is an important part of the laundry process. If loads are dried properly in a dryer according to the manufacturer's directions, many articles will be quite wrinkle-free. When it is especially desirable to minimize wrinkling, articles should be removed immediately after the dryer stops regardless of the fiber content of the fabrics. Any residual moisture in warm items piled together will help press in wrinkles. Even the cooling period which is provided in a wash-and-wear cycle does not completely eliminate the problem. If garments are placed on hangers immediately after removal from the dryer, collars, pockets, and trim can be straightened.

Many homemakers still prefer to air-dry garments when possible. In some cases, drip-drying can minimize or eliminate ironing. Drip-drying means that a garment is removed from the rinse water before the final spin cycle of the washer and hung to dry without being spun, wrung, twisted, or squeezed in any way. The lack of a convenient place to drip-dry limits the use of this method.

Hand Laundering

Many types of items once laundered by hand may now be laundered in an automatic washer.

Very delicate fabrics, loosely woven wools, some knitted fabrics, and some fiber glass may need to be hand washed. Fabrics labeled as machine-washable may be laundered according to the manufacturer's directions.

Garments that are not colorfast or have fragile ornamentation or seams that may pull apart in laundering require special handling. Hang tags or labels often give recommendations for washing.

For hand washing, the water temperature should be comfortable to the hands. The soap or detergent should be dissolved completely before garments are put into the water. Suds should be squeezed carefully through the fabric.

Rinsing should be done in two or more waters. Water may be squeezed out, and additional water can be pressed out by rolling the items in a bath towel and patting.

If colors have a tendency to run, items should be rolled in a terry towel to absorb excess moisture, then hung in front of a fan or in a breeze to speed drying and prevent dye transfer.

Fabrics which are to be drip-dried should be hung without squeezing or wringing. They will be less wrinkled and retain their original shape better if they are handled or hung so that wrinkles are not formed.

No one method is right for every washable garment. No overall statement can be made on types of garments which can be washed, or which must be washed by hand. All textile items which require any type of special handling should carry adequate instructions on labels or hang tags. These should be saved and manufacturer's recommendations followed.

Home Laundering (Continued)

Ironing

Not all fabrics need to be ironed. Terry cloth, plissé crepe, and many fabrics of the man-made fibers can be finger pressed or smoothed by hand if they have been properly laundered. New finishes for cotton are also eliminating or reducing the need for ironing.

Proper temperature is the most important consideration in hand ironing of fabrics. This is particularly true with man-made thermoplastic fibers which can be damaged or melted and destroyed at temperatures far below those that are safe for cotton or linen. Resin and other finishes for both man-made and natural fibers have influenced the temperatures at which fabrics may be ironed.

In order to guide the consumer in using an appropriate temperature in ironing or pressing fabrics, manufacturers may provide some ironing instructions on the labels of textile articles. The manufacturers of household ironing equipment have installed thermostats on their equipment and adjust these to provide controlled temperatures suitable for the various fibers. At present, there is no standard terminology for thermostat settings, and the temperature range for the various fabric settings may vary somewhat.

If the consumer has any doubt about the temperature at which an item can be ironed safely, she should begin at a low temperature and gradually increase it if necessary. When ironing fabrics made of blends of several fibers, she should use the setting for the most sensitive fiber. If the garment has been dampened, a slightly higher temperature may be used.

Garments may be ironed dry, dampened before ironing, or dampened during ironing with moisture supplied by a steam or spray iron. Dampening before ironing may be done by hand, or automatically in a dryer.

Light but even dampening will speed ironing. Warm water penetrates more quickly than cold, so that ironing can be done an hour after dampening. Storing damp items in a plastic bag encourages even dampening and keeps clothes damp for several days. The bag should be stored in a cold place to avoid mildew.

A few generalizations can be made about the need for dampening or steam, but experience with each individual item to be ironed is necessary to determine whether moisture is needed and if so, the amount needed Until recent years, cotton, linen, rayon, and other absorbent fibers were dampened with little question. Today, wrinkle-resistant-finished fabrics frequently require only steam ironing. Tablecloths, sheets, and other items which ordinarily do not have a finish still need thorough dampening. Many man-made fiber fabrics are satisfactorily ironed with a steam iron.

Natural fibers should be ironed until completely dry. Man-made fabrics should be slightly damp. Seams and double thicknesses should be thoroughly dry to prevent puckering. (This discussion does not apply to wool because it is pressed, not ironed.) Ironing on the wrong side under seams prevents seam edges from showing on the right side.

Fabrics should not be ironed on the right side if ironing produces a shine. These fabrics, as well as dark cottons, linens, silks, and rayons, are usually ironed on the wrong side. The right side of the garment can be touched up where needed (as on pockets or collars) with iron and a press cloth. If a surface has a raised effect, it should be ironed on a pad from the wrong side.

For ironing garments with curved surfaces, a press mitt is helpful, especially in the shoulder area. The pad should be fluffed periodically to insure smooth ironing. The cover should be washed and kept free of scorch marks. Sleeves may be pressed without a crease on a sleeve board or roll. The elasticized portions of garments or fabrics which are waterproofed with waxes, rubber, or other coatings that may melt easily should not be ironed.

Organization of equipment and procedure will speed ironing. Recommended ironing techniques give best results and increase speed, particularly when an automatic ironer is used.

Spot and Stain Removal

General Instructions

• Treat the stain promptly—before it dries, if possible. Fresh stains react better than old ones.

• Before using any stain remover on colored clothes, first experiment with a sample from the seam or some other inconspicuous section.

- If a garment is in need of overall cleaning, do not try to treat isolated stains. The result will be a clean area unsightly by contrast.
- If in doubt about what caused the stain, try only cool water and cleaning fluid or powder. Sponge with the cool water first and then let fabric dry before applying the cleaning fluid.
- Always work from the under side of the stain to avoid driving the stain through the fabric.

Stain Identification

Of first importance in spot and stain removal is stain identification. Stains may be identified by observing:

Appearance. The *color* of a stain helps to identify it (red coloring of a lipstick stain, brown coloring of iodine stain). So does the *form* of a stain on a fabric surface (ink penetrates surface, paint builds up on a surface). *Shape* should also be observed. For example, oil stains follow the yarns with the least degree of twist. If yarns are of equal twist in both warp and filling, a perfect cross will appear.

Odor. Odor is frequently a tell-tale sign that may identify perfume, cold-wave solution (faint odor of bromine), or medicinal stains.

Location may indicate the type of stain (perspiration in the underarm areas of a suit or blouse, food stains on ties or dress and suit fronts).

Feel. The texture of a stain helps to identify it. Egg, a type of albuminous stain, may be recognized by its stiffness; glue and adhesives are sticky; paint may be rough or smooth; fingernail polish may feel built up on fabric surface.

Stain Classification

After a stain is identified, it should be classified as to whether it is removable with a dry solvent or with a water solution. The following list illustrates classification of stains and type of removal agent.

Stains removed with dry solvents: Carbon black (complete removal difficult), dry inks (ballpoint and marking inks), gum, nail polish, oils, paints, plastic base adhesives

Stains removed with water solutions: *Albumin* (animal glues, blood, cream, egg, gelatin, ice cream, milk); *dye stains* (berry stains, leather dyes, Mercurochrome®, Merthiolate®, wet writing inks); *reducing sugars* (fruit juices, liquor, soft drinks, and drink mixes); *tannin* (beer, coffee, grass, tannic acid, tea, tobacco, walnut stains)

Methods of Stain Removal

Solvent action occurs when one substance is dissolved in another. For example: Sugar dissolves in water. The mechanical action of stirring hastens the solvent action on the sugar. Sugar is not soluble in drycleaning solvents, and no amount of stirring will dissolve the sugar.

Thus in stain removal a suitable solvent must be selected for each type of soluble substance that is in the stain. If the wrong solvent is used, no amount of mechanical action will remove the stain.

Lubrication is a very important method of stain and soil removal, particularly in removing insoluble and chemically inactive substances. An illustration of the physical action of lubrication is typified by the washing of mud from fabric in water. The soil is not dissolved but dislodged by lubrication.

Chemical Action. There are some stains which must be removed by chemical action. However, these stains are in the minority. In such instances, a chemical spot-remover reacts with the stain or substance in such a manner as to produce a new compound. The compound does not have any characteristics of either the original stain or spotting reagent, and may be rendered invisible or soluble and easily flushed from the fabric. For example: An iodine stain treated with ammonia will result in the formation of ammonium iodide, which is a colorless water-soluble substance that can be rinsed from the fabric.

Digestion. Many stains require digestion for removal. There are now enzyme presoaking products and enzyme detergents available for home use which will handle these types of stains. Enzymes have also long been used by commercial dry cleaners.

Precautions in Stain Removal

Several precautions should be kept in mind in approaching any stain removal problem:

STAIN AND SPOT REMOVAL CHART

Type of Stain	Machine- and Hand-Washable Fabrics	Others
Beverages (Alcoholic and Soft Drinks)	Soak in cold water, wash in warm sudsy water, rinse. If stain remains, soak silk, wool, or colored items for half hour in 2 tablespoons hydrogen peroxide to 1 gallon water. Launder. Soak white linen, rayon, and cotton 15 minutes in 1 tablespoon household bleach to 1 quart water. Launder.	Take to drycleaner. Identify stain for drycleaner's information.
Blood	Soak in lukewarm water and enzyme-containing, pre-soak or detergent product. Launder.	Treat with cold water to which table salt has been added (2 tablespoons per quart of water). Salt helps prevent color bleeding. Rinse and blot with towel.
Candle Wax	Remove surface wax with dull knife. Place towel under stain, wet thoroughly several times with cleaning fluid. Dry and launder. Use chlorine bleach if color of candle remains and fabric is bleachable.	Remove surface wax with dull knife. Sponge with cleaning fluid.
Chewing Gum	Remove gum from surface with dull knife. Soak affected areas in cleaning fluid. Launder.	Same as for washable fabrics, but do not launder.
Chocolate or Coffee	Soak in warm water with enzyme-containing product. Launder.	If fabric is colorfast, sponge with luke-warm water.
Deodorants (Cream, stick, or spray variety)	Wash in solution of detergent, chlorine bleach, and hot water.	Sponge with drycleaning solvent.
Fruit and Berry	Soak using an enzyme-containing product. Launder. If stain remains, use chlorine bleach. Rinse thoroughly.	Treat with cold water.

STAIN AND SPOT REMOVAL CHART (Cont.)

Type of Stain	Machine- and Hand-Washable Fabrics	Others
Grass	Soak using an enzyme-containing product. Wash in detergent. Bleach if necessary.	Take to drycleaner.
Grease and Tar	Place towel under stain. Pour cleaning fluid through stained area. Launder in hot water.	Take to drycleaner. Identify stain for drycleaner's information.
Ink	Pour water through stained area; repeat if bleeding of ink continues. If stain does not bleed, dry the treated area and then wet with water. Apply detergent and white vinegar. Rinse. Launder. A patented rust remover is also useful on ink stains and may be tried either alone or in combination with above treatment. Rinse thoroughly. Apply household ammonia. Rinse. Bleach remaining traces with laundry bleach. Launder.	Take to drycleaner. Identify stain for drycleaner's information.
Ink, ball-point pen	Place blotter under fabric. Drip home drycleaning solvent through spot. Soak in solution of detergent and warm water. Rinse in cold water. Use mild bleach, but test fabric first. Launder.	Take to drycleaner. Identify stain as ball-point ink variety.
Lipstick	Turn garment inside out and place stained area over absorbent towel. Pour cleaning fluid slowly through stained area until bleeding stops. Dry. Launder with detergent in hot water.	Same as for washable fabric. Apply cleaning fluid treatment only.

Stain	Washable	Dry-cleanable
Mildew	Launder with detergent and chlorine bleach if color and fabric permit.	Take to drycleaner. Identify stain for drycleaner's information.
Milk, Cream, and Ice Cream	Soak in warm water with enzyme-containing product. Launder.	Sponge with cleaning fluid. If stain remains and fabric is colorfast, sponge stain lightly with tepid water.
Mud	Allow to dry. Brush lightly. Launder.	Dry and brush.
Paint	Use solvent recommended on paint label as thinner. Sponge with this fluid as soon as possible. Pretreat with detergent and launder.	Take to drycleaner. Identify stain for drycleaner's information.
Perfume or Cologne	Wash immediately in solution of detergent and hot water; don't let stain age. Bleach if necessary.	Take to drycleaner. Identify stain for drycleaner's information.
Perspiration	Launder with detergent in hot water. Bleach if necessary.	Sponge with water if fabric is color-fast.
Rust	Apply patented rust remover as manufacturer directs. Launder.	Take to drycleaner. Identify stain for drycleaner's information.
Shoe Polish, liquid	Sponge with denatured alcohol. Launder with detergent in hot water. Bleach if necessary	Take to drycleaner. Identify stain for drycleaner's information.
Tea	Launder. Bleach if necessary.	Sponge with water if fabric is color-fast.
Water Spots	Launder.	Wipe very lightly with damp cloth.

*Mercurochrome® is a registered trademark of Hynson, Westcott and Dunning, Incorporated; Merthiolate® is a registered trademark of Eli Lilly and Company; Metaphen® is a registered trademark of Abbott Laboratories.

Precautions in Stain Removal (Continued)

Stains on washable fabrics are removed at home more easily than are stains on drycleanable fabrics. When there is a question about one's ability to cope with a stain, a drycleaner should be consulted.

Effects of water on drycleaning fluid should be tested on a sample of fabric before attempt is made to remove a spot or stain from a garment.

Chlorine bleach, hydrogen peroxide, or any other bleach should not be used on colored fabrics except when the colors are known to be truly fast to such treatment. Chlorine bleach should not be used on silk or wool fabrics, or on some resin-treated fabrics. White acetate may be bleached if bleach is diluted according to manufacturer's directions.

Stained fabrics should not be pressed. The heat of pressing causes many stains to become permanently set.

A built-up stain should be removed as much as possible by scraping before spotting fluid is applied. Care should be taken not to injure the fabric.

Old remedies, such as applying milk to ink stains, are unreliable. Milk can be more difficult to remove than ink.

A clean soft cloth such as cheesecloth should be used to apply the spotting fluid. White blotting paper or terry cloth toweling should be used under the area to be spotted to absorb the spotting fluid and staining substance as it is flushed from the fabric.

If fabric has a tendency to ring, the best procedure is to brush lightly and rapidly from the center of the wet area to the outer edge and one or two inches beyond and continue until the ring disappears.

Cleaning products should be used and stored carefully according to directions and precautions given by the manufacturer.

Stain Removal Compounds

The types of household detergents best suited to stain removal work are liquids such as Wisk, All, or liquid dishwashing detergents. However, a solution of any laundry detergent can be used satisfactorily.

When it is necessary to use an oxidizing bleach on white or colorfast fabrics (except for silk, wool, or fabrics with chlorine-retentive finishes), chlorine bleaches, sodium perborate, or hydrogen peroxide may be used. Sodium perborate, sodium monopersulfate, and hydrogen peroxide can generally be used interchangeably, but sodium perborate has the advantage of greater stability in storage and, when feasible the action of the bleach can be speeded up by use of the bleach with very hot water. Chlorine bleaches will sometimes remove stains not removed by the peroxygen bleaches.

A patented preparation containing rust-removing chemicals may be bought at a drugstore for treatment of ink and rust stains.

White vinegar is an inexpensive source of acetic acid, which is often required either to neutralize alkaline conditions or cause a necessary reaction with the stain. White vinegar will not harm any fabric that can withstand water.

Carbon tetrachloride is not recommended as a cleaning fluid for home use because of the danger in working with it. Solvents such as trichlorethylene and perchlorethylene are less toxic solvents that may be used for spot removal.

Following is a partial list of stain removal compounds and the types of stains for which they are intended. Italics indicate brand names with manufacturer in parentheses. (See Appendix for complete names and addresses.)

For general stains: *Energine* (d-Con Co.); *Renuzit* (Renuzit); laundry bleaches; 3-percent, 10-volume hydrogen peroxide

For grease and oil: *Carbona* (Carbona)

For light greasy stains: Perchlorethylene; trichlorethylene

For ink, soft drinks, alcoholic beverages: Glycerine

For nail polish: Acetone (Do *not* use on acetate fabrics)

Stain Removal Procedures

There are many procedures used in removing stains. Not all are applicable to all fibers. The accompanying chart suggests methods of dealing with the more common types of stains. If there is any doubt about possible success, however, a professionally trained person should be consulted even for washable fabrics. This may save and protect the value of the entire garment.

Textile Labeling

There are three basic reasons for labeling textile merchandise: (1) to identify the product; (2) to aid the businessman in selling his product; (3) to aid the consumer in making an intelligent selection.

Textiles in the forms in which they reach the retailer and consumer may be labeled in various ways, such as (1) printed identification on the bolt or roller, spool, or wrapper; (2) identification woven into or printed on the selvage; (3) printed label pasted onto the item; (4) hang tag attached to the item; (5) woven or printed label permanently attached.

Garments are usually labeled by one or both of the following: (1) a cardboard hang tag attached to the garment. This type of label can carry factual and promotional information. It is easily removed.

(2) A ribbon or cloth label machine-stitched in a seam or on a facing of the garment.

Other permanent labeling may be accomplished by stamping information on the garment, as sizes on men's shirts and brand and size on fabric gloves.

Types of Labels

The information provided on either a printed or woven label may fall under any of the following three classifications:

Brand

This type of label is a distinctive mark, design, symbol, word, or combination of these, used to identify the goods of a particular seller, a single design or "line" of a manufacturer. Trademark names fall in this type of labeling.

Certification

Such labels indicate that an item has been tested by a laboratory, usually one independent of the manufacturer of the product. Each laboratory may establish its own fixed standard of quality. Such labels are often referred to as "seals of approval" labels. Usually no information is given on the label except that the article has been approved or guaranteed by a particular laboratory or agency.

An article manufactured according to recognized standards, such as those of the American National Standards Institute, may also bear a label indicating that it meets these standards. This, too, would be a certification label, since in the process of setting up the standards, it was determined that all articles manufactured or processed in accordance with the standards would have certain characteristics.

Informative

In general, informative labels should state fiber content, fabric structure, special finishes that affect serviceability, directions and precautions on proper use and care, and, in addition, size of the item and the manufacturer's name and address.

Much of this type of labeling is required by law, either through an Act such as the Textile Fiber Products Identification Act and subsequent Amendment or a Trade Regulation Rule similar to the one on permanent care labeling. (See chapter on **Textile Legislation and Trade Rules and Regulations,** pages 101 to 105.)

Control of Labeling

Both consumer and producer benefit from various types of legal protection in the area of labeling. Brand names and trademark names are protected by law, and only the person or firm that has properly registered the trademark or trademark name is entitled to its use. Trademarks are registered with the U. S. Patent Office.

Legislation specifying that certain information about textile products must be provided to the consumer—and in some instances to purchasers and users at various stages of the manufacturing process—not only protects the consumer but assures him of having part of the information he needs for a wise decision. By requiring accurate labeling, the legislation also protects the ethical businessman from unfair competition.

Textile Standards

Textile standards provide a blueprint for the manufacture of products that will give a guaranteed and predictable performance or make it possible to duplicate a certain product exactly. Standards also provide a common performance-language and a common yardstick, so to speak, by which similar products can be measured. Performance standards are based on standard test methods and on evaluation of results that indicate a quality acceptable for the product.

Standards in the textile field are of interest to many groups in the manufacturing and distribution of textiles, to government purchasing agencies, to technical and professional societies, and to the ultimate consumer of the textile products. Many of these groups have established certain standards for their own use.

Some large department stores, mail-order houses, chain stores, and buying groups, have standards that aid the retailer in providing merchandise acceptable to his customers and help him avoid complaints and expensive returns of unsatisfactory products. A manufacturer may set up a standards program to help him develop quality products; he can also refer to these standards in selling his product. (Such a standards program was established by the American Viscose Company; it later formed the basis for part of the rayon and acetate standards which evolved into L22 standards established in 1952 by the American Standards Association, now the American National Standards Institute.)

In contrast to mandatory labeling of fiber content of fabrics as required by law, standards are often optional or voluntary. Exceptions are the mandatory flammability standards for specified fabrics and consumer items. (See **Flammable Fabrics Act,** p. 103.)

In general, the manufacturer is free to produce textile items that do or do not meet standards, but once he indicates that his products are meeting certain standards, the products must, in fact, meet these standards. If not, he is guilty of false advertising.

American National Standards

An *American national standard* is a voluntary national standard approved by the American National Standards Institute, Inc. (ANSI). The Institute is a nonprofit federation of trade, technical, labor, and consumer organizations, companies, and government agencies. Its purpose is to provide systematic means by which organizations concerned with standardization work may cooperate in establishing American national standards to avoid duplication of work and the promulgation of conflicting standards. Before the Institute approves a proposed standard, its provisions must be acceptable to the national groups affected.

The standards set forth certain minimum requirements that do not regiment or place limitations on aesthetic elements but establish a quality base below which the listed textile products should not fall.

Two major textile standards, established by ANSI, are L22-1968 on performance requirements for textile fabrics, first sponsored by the National Retail Merchants Association, and L24-1963 on minimum performance requirements for institutional textiles, sponsored by the American Hotel and Motel Association.

In 1973, the L22 committee voted to dissolve its affiliation with ANSI and to affiliate instead with the American Society for Testing and Materials (ASTM).

For more detailed information on *American national standards* for textiles, write to the American National Standards Institute, Inc., 1430 Broadway, New York, New York, 10018.

Federal Government

Product Standards (National Bureau of Standards of the U. S. Department of Commerce)

The Office of Engineering Standards Services of the National Bureau of Standards assists industry—manufacturers, distributors, and users—

in the development of *product standards* for a wide variety of products, many of them in the textile field. *Product standards* are concerned primarily with quality criteria for materials, dimensions, tolerances, grading, marking, and labeling. They may also establish standard test methods, common stock items, and standard sizes for a variety of purposes. These standards are voluntary, but because they are generally requested by an industry, they soon become established trade practice.

Although the request for a standard and its initial development may be sponsored by a group representing a single segment of an industry, final development and any revisions are the responsibility of a committee representing all segments of an industry. The procedure for the approval of a standard is based on the consensus principle. Before a new standard is approved, it must be accepted by a significant portion of the industry concerned, including producers, distributors, users, and consumers, as well as state and federal agencies.

Product standards were formerly known as *commercial standards* which were developed under the same general procedures. As any existing commercial standards are revised, they will be identified as product standards. For additional textile standards information from the Department of Commerce write to National Bureau of Standards, Washington, D.C. 20234, or Office of Textiles, BDSA, U. S. Department of Commerce, Washington, D.C. 20230.

Federal Specifications and Standards

Federal specifications and standards are promulgated by the Standardization Division, Federal Supply Service, General Services Administration. These documents indicate physical and chemical requirements and applicable test methods for controlling the quality of textile and apparel items used by two or more federal agencies. This does not include, however, items considered to be strictly military or special service items. These documents are mandatory for use by all federal agencies and are available to the public.

Departmental Specifications and Standards

Departmental specifications and standards for textile and apparel items are developed and issued by individual federal agencies primarily for their own use, but may also be used by other agencies. Copies of these standards and specifications may be obtained from the respective agencies.

Copies of *military and federal specifications and standards, qualified products lists, military handbooks,* etc., listed in the Department of Defense Index of Specifications and Standards (DODISS) can be obtained from Commanding Officer, Naval Publications and Forms Center, 5801 Tabor Avenue, Philadelphia, Pennsylvania 19120.

American Home Economics Association

The American Home Economics Association's interest in textile standards is expressed through its representation on the L12, L14, L22, L23, and L24 committees of the American National Standards Institute, Inc., and on the Institute's Textile Standards Board as well as through its cooperation in publicizing and promoting American national standards.

The Association also cooperates with various other technical and research organizations in an effort to recommend and establish minimum standards for clothing and textiles, and has given continuous support to programs for consumer protection in the Federal Trade Commission and other government agencies.

International Organization for Standardization

The International Organization for Standardization (sometimes designated as ISO) deals with industrial and engineering standards other than electrical. Members of ISO are national standards organizations of countries desiring to participate. The United States is represented by the American National Standards Institute.

As a nongovernmental organization, ISO has been accorded consultative status by the Economic and Social Council of the United Nations. The administrative work is handled by the Central Secretariat, located in Geneva, Switzerland. Proposed standards are developed and agreed upon by an ISO technical committee, a draft is circulated to member bodies, and when approved by 60 percent of the members voting, it becomes an official *ISO recommendation*. The ISO recommendations, like the American national standards, are voluntary.

ISO recommendations in the fields of colorfastness, dimensional stability, and other performance characteristics of fabrics, yarn testing, and fiber testing are under development with the active participation of the United States. About 15 ISO textiles recommendations have been approved.

Test Method Standards

Test methods, which leading technical societies have developed, provide nationally recognized and reproducible methods that are widely used in textile research and testing and are the basis for establishing textile performance requirements. Two such recognized organizations [1] are mentioned here:

American Association of Textile Chemists and Colorists

The AATCC is a national technical and scientific body whose members are active in the textile wet-processing industry. The Association's object is to promote increase of knowledge of the application of dyes and chemicals in the textile industry, to encourage research work on chemical processes and materials of importance to the industry, and to promote exchange of professional knowledge among its members. This Association develops many tests, particularly in the area of chemical testing and sponsors workshops, symposiums, and seminars on test methods.

The proceedings of AATCC are published in its own journal, *Textile Chemist and Colorist*. The Association's test methods and other technical information are published in the annual *Technical Manual*. Most AATCC test methods have been approved as American national standards in the L14 (textile test method) series.

American Society for Testing and Materials

The purpose of this society is to "promote knowledge of the materials of engineering, and the standardization of specifications and the methods of testing." [2] The Society's *Book of ASTM Standards*, issued annually, contains all of its current standard tests for textiles as well as a section entitled, Standard Definitions of Terms Relating to Textile Materials. This information, formerly contained in Parts 24 and 25, will now be found in Parts 32 and 33 of the 1974 edition.

The ASTM is usually looked to for physical tests and for tests dealing with fabric construction which form the basis for the specifications appearing in American national standard L24. Many ASTM standards in the D (textiles) category have been approved as American national standards in the L14 (textile test method) series.

---

[1] See Appendix for addresses.

[2] From ASTM Charter, March 21, 1902.

Textile Legislation and Trade Rules and Regulations

Since 1939, Congress has enacted four textile and fur laws and a product safety act designed for consumer protection. These are:

The Wool Products Labeling Act of 1939 as amended to 1965

The Fur Products Labeling Act of 1951 as amended to 1969

The Textile Fiber Products Identification Act of 1958 as amended to 1969

The Flammable Fabrics Act as amended to 1967

The Consumer Product Safety Act of 1972

The wool, fur, and textile fiber products acts are designed to protect consumers and producers alike against misbranding and false advertising of textiles and furs and are administered by the Federal Trade Commission's Bureau of Textiles and Furs. The Flammable Fabrics Act prohibits the introduction or movement in interstate commerce of wearing apparel, interior furnishings, and related products that are so flammable as to present *"unreasonable"* risk or hazard to the consumer. The provisions of this act have been subsumed by the Consumer Product Safety Act of 1972 which is administered by the Consumer Product Safety Commission, independent of other agency.

Legislation

Wool Products Labeling Act of 1939 (approved October 14, 1940, Public Law No. 850, 76th Congress, 3rd Session; 15 U.S.C. § 68, 54 Stat. 1128) as amended to 1965

This Act provides for mandatory fiber content labeling by percentages of all fibers present in all products containing wool, reprocessed wool, or reused wool fibers in any amount. It also generally prohibits false or deceptive labels on woolen products. Fiber content labels must accompany woolen products from their raw-fiber stage through the various processes of manufacture and distribution until the end product reaches the consumer.

The Federal Trade Commission has issued 36 rules and regulations for industry guidance under the Act.

Definitions. The following definitions are included in the Wool Products Labeling Act:

Wool means the fiber from the fleece of the sheep or lamb or hair of the Angora or Cashmere goat (and may include the so-called specialty fibers from the hair of the camel, alpaca, llama, and vicuña) which has never been reclaimed from any woven or felted wool product.

Reprocessed wool means the resulting fiber when wool has been woven, or felted into a wool product which, without ever having been utilized in any way by the ultimate consumer, subsequently has been made into a fibrous state.

Reused wool means the resulting fiber when wool or reprocessed wool has been spun, woven, knitted, or felted into a wool product which, after having been used in any way by the ultimate consumer, subsequently has been made into a fibrous state.

Wool product means any product, or any portion of a product, which contains, purports to contain, or in any way is represented as containing wool, reprocessed wool, or reused wool.

The law does not require that specialty fibers (angora, cashmere, camel, etc.) be indicated by name on labels, since they may be labeled as wool but where they are named, the percentage must be given. If the specialty fibers have been reprocessed or reused, this information must be stated on the label.

Effectiveness. According to the Federal Trade Commission, required fiber content disclosure, by percentages, has practically eliminated the use of such general terms as "woolen" and "part-wool" in describing products which contain little or no wool at all.

The practice of using reused wool without disclosing its presence in fabrics has greatly diminished since the passage of the Act. The incentive to use substitute fibers in lieu of more costly wool fibers has also lessened in view of the affirmative labeling requirements. Also, a once common practice of passing off inferior quality fibers has been curbed as a result of the legislation.

Carpets, rugs, mats and upholsteries are exempted from the provisions of the Act.

Fur Products Labeling Act (approved August 8, 1951, Public Law 110, 82nd Congress, 1st Session; 15 U.S.C.A. § 69; 65 Stat. 179) as amended to 1969

The Fur Products Labeling Act requires that purchasers be informed on labels, invoices, and in advertising of the true English name of the animal from which the fur came, its country of origin, and whether the fur product is composed of used, damaged, or scrap fur, or fur that has been dyed or bleached. The Act further requires that the terminology in the *Fur Products Name Guide*, amended in 1967 and issued by the Federal Trade Commission, be used in setting forth the animal name. A 1969 amendment to the Act added further provisions in the regulation of furs that are pointed, dyed, bleached, or otherwise artificially colored. The FTC rules prohibit the use of fictitious prices in labeling and advertising.

Definitions. The following definitions are included in the Fur Products Labeling Act:

Fur means any animal skin or part thereof with hair, fleece, or fur fibers attached thereto, either in its raw or processed state, but shall not include such skins as are to be converted into leather or which in processing shall have the hair, fleece, or fur fiber completely removed.

Used fur means fur in any form which has been worn or used by an ultimate consumer.

Fur product means any article of wearing apparel made in whole or in part of fur or used fur; except that such term shall not include such

articles as the Commission shall exempt by reason of the relatively small quantity or value of the fur or used fur contained therein.

Waste fur means the ears, throats, or scrap pieces which have been severed from the animal pelt, and shall include mats and plates made therefrom.

Effectiveness. According to the Federal Trade Commission, requiring accurate information about furs on labels, invoices, etc., has helped to eliminate deceptive practices in the fur trade.

Textile Fiber Products Identification Act (approved September 2, 1958, 85th Congress, 2nd Session; 15 U.S.C. § 70, 72 Stat. 1717) as amended to 1969

This Act requires mandatory fiber content labeling by percentages of all textile fiber products and covers textiles used for wearing apparel, costumes, and accessories, as well as draperies, floor coverings, furnishings, bedding, and other textile goods of a type customarily used in a household regardless of the place where used.

Definitions. The following textile definitions are included in the Textile Products Identification Act:

Fiber or *textile fiber* means a unit of matter which is capable of being spun into a yarn or made into a fabric by bonding or by interlacing in a variety of methods including weaving, knitting, braiding, felting, twisting, or webbing, and which is the basic structural element of textile products.

Natural fiber means any fiber that exists as such in the natural state.

Manufactured fiber means any fiber derived by a process of manufacture from any substance which, at any point in the manufacturing process, is not a fiber.

Fabric means any material woven, knitted, felted, or otherwise produced from, or in combination with, any natural or manufactured fiber, yarn, or substitute therefor.

Yarn means a strand of textile fiber in a form suitable for weaving, knitting, braiding, felting, webbing, or otherwise fabricating into a fabric.

Textile fiber product means: (1) any fiber, whether in the finished or unfinished state, used or intended for use in household textile articles;

Textile Fiber Products Identification Act—
Definitions (Continued)

(2) any yarn or fabric, whether in the finished or unfinished state, used or intended for use in household textile articles; and (3) any household textile article made in whole or in part of yarn or fabric; except that such term does not include a product required to be labeled under the Wool Products Labeling Act of 1939.

The Act provides that a stamp, tag, label, or other means of identification giving the following information must be affixed to textile fiber products subject to the Act:

(1) *The constituent fiber or combination of fibers* in the textile fiber product, designating with equal prominence each natural or manufactured fiber by its generic name in the order of predominance by weight if the weight is five percent or more of the total fiber weight.

(2) *The percentage of each fiber present,* by weight, in the total fiber content. Individual fibers in amounts less than five percent by weight may not be designated by fiber names, but must be shown as "other fibers." Exception: Where a textile fiber is present in a textile fiber product in an amount less than five percent and it is clearly established that such fiber has a definite functional significance, the fiber may be identified by its generic name provided the functional significance is also stated on the label. Ornamentation not exceeding five percent of the total fiber weight need not be disclosed, provided that the phrase "exclusive of ornamentation" accompanies the designation.

(3) If an upholstered product, mattress, or cushion contains *stuffing which previously has been used as stuffing* in any other upholstered product, mattress or cushion, there must be a statement to this effect.

(4) *The name or other identification of the manufacturer* of the product or one or more persons subject to the Act.

(5) For *imported textile fiber products,* the name of the country where the product was processed or manufactured must be disclosed along with the required content and identification disclosures.

The Federal Trade Commission has established the following 19 generic names for classes of manmade fibers:

acetate	glass	nytril	saran
acrylic	metallic	olefin	spandex
anidex	modacrylic	polyester	vinal
aramid	novoloid	rayon	vinyon
azlon	nylon	rubber	

The FTC definitions for these classes appear in the section entitled *Textile Fibers.*

Definitions were drafted on the basis of the broad chemical composition of each class of fibers as they are currently manufactured.

Each generic name covers a class of fibers which may differ more or less widely in properties, just as the names "wool" and "cotton" cover fibers that differ widely in value, properties, and serviceability. Any difference in the characteristics and their effect on the suitability of a fiber for any particular end-use is a matter for the manufacturer or seller to explain in informational materials and in advertising. The object of the generic name and definition is to identify the fiber-forming substance in the particular class of fiber, rather than on the basis of quality. These generic names must also be used in labeling products subject to the Wool Products Labeling Act.

The Federal Trade Commission urges consumers to become familiar with the generic names of manufactured fibers and to learn the advantages and disadvantages of each in the interest of wise consumer buying.

Flammable Fabrics Act (approved June 30, 1953, Public Law 88, 83rd Congress, 1st Session; 15 U.S.C.A. § 1191; 67 Stat. 111) as amended to 1967

The original Act of 1953 as amended in 1954 specified that the standards to be used for determining dangerously flammable materials for apparel should be those presented in "the Commercial Standard promulgated by the Secretary of Commerce effective January 30, 1953 . . ." All wearing apparel, regardless of material, fiber content, or construction, fell within the provisions of the Act. Also included were fabrics and films sold and intended for use in apparel. The legislation prohibited importation or marketing in interstate commerce of fabrics or wearing apparel that failed to meet the prescribed standards.

The 1967 Amendments in effect continued these standards and regulations unless revised by the Secretary of Commerce or superseded by later standards and regulations. The legislation also authorized research on flammability; development of test methods and devices; the training of personnel; and continuing investigation of deaths, injuries, and economic losses that resulted from accidental burning of fabrics, related materials, or products.

Under the 1967 Amendments, the Secretary of Commerce promulgated four flammability standards as follows:

(1) DOC FF 1-70, Standard for Carpets and Rugs, which was issued April 1970 and became effective April 1971.

(2) DOC FF 2-70, Standard for Small Carpets and Rugs, which was issued December 1970 and became effective December 1971.

(3) DOC FF 3-71, Standard for Children's Sleepwear, Sizes 0-6X, which was issued July, 1971. It became effective in two steps with the first step occurring in July 1972 and the second in July 1973.

(4) DOC FF 4-72, Standard for Mattresses, which was issued in June 1972 and became effective June 1973. However, amendments allowed a delay in full compliance until December 1973.

In addition, the Commerce Department published findings that standards might be needed for blankets, upholstered furniture, and children's sleepwear (sizes 7-14). Proposed standards are being or have been developed for these uses but have not been promulgated to date.

Three agencies—the Department of Health, Education, and Welfare, the Commerce Department, and the Federal Trade Commission—formerly administered certain provisions of the Act. Responsibility has since been transferred. (See **Consumer Product Safety Act.**)

Effectiveness. The original Act effectively barred from the marketplace wearing apparel fabrics of extremely hazardous flammability. However, the burning of common wearing apparel and interior furnishing not covered by the Act and Amendments continued to cause several hundreds of deaths annually. The 1967 Amendments increased the protection of the public against potentially unsafe fabrics in the specific end-use items of carpets and rugs, children's sleepwear (0-6X), and mattresses.

Consumer Product Safety Act (approved October 27, 1972, Public Law 92-573, 92nd Congress, 2nd Session)

The purposes of this Act are: (1) to protect the public against unreasonable risks of injury associated with consumer products; (2) to assist consumers in evaluating the comparative safety of consumer products; (3) to develop uniform safety standards for consumer products and to minimize conflicting state and local regulations; and (4) to promote research and investigation into the causes and prevention of product-related deaths, illnesses, and injuries. The Act requires the formation of a five-member commission to supervise and implement the provisions of the Act which include administration of the Flammable Fabrics Act as amended to 1967.

In this connection, the Act transfers certain responsibilities of other agencies to the Consumer Product Safety Commission. These are: the functions of the Secretary of Health, Education, and Welfare in gathering data on deaths, injuries, and economic losses caused by flammable fabrics; those of the Secretary of Commerce in developing and promulgating needed flammability standards; plus the functions of the Federal Trade Commission in enforcing federal flammability standards. Thus, investigation to determine need for new fabric flammability standards, development of standards, and their enforcement are now concentrated in one agency instead of being distributed among three agencies. Hopefully, this will increase the effectiveness of the Flammable Fabrics Act.

The Commission members were appointed during 1973. They are currently working toward new standards for children's sleepwear (sizes 7-14) and for upholstered furniture.

Rules and Regulations

To carry out certain provisions of the textile and fur laws, the Federal Trade Commission was empowered to promulgate rules and regulations necessary and proper for enforcement of these statutes.

Rules having the force and effect of law are authorized under Section 6 of the Wool Products Labeling Act of 1939, Section 8 of the Fur Products Labeling Act, and Section 7 of the Textile Fiber Products Identification Act.

The Commission also issues trade regulation rules applicable to unlawful trade practices when in the experience and judgment of the Commission such rules are necessary to fulfill the substantive requirements of the statutes.

In December, 1971, the Federal Trade Commission issued a Trade Regulation Rule requiring that wearing apparel (with some exceptions) carry a permanently affixed care label and that a care label be given to buyers of piece goods intended for conversion into wearing apparel. In essence, the rule requires that care labels:

(1) give full, clear information on the regular care and maintenance of the article

(2) warn the purchaser about any regular care and maintenance procedures that might normally be expected to apply to such an article but which, if used, would substantially decrease its ordinary use and the wearer's enjoyment of the article

(3) be easy to locate and remain legible for the useful life of the article

(4) omit symbols unless accompanied by word descriptions.

This Trade Rule Regulation became effective July 3, 1972.

Proceedings for the issuance of rules or regulations, including proceedings for exemption of products or classes of products from statutory requirements, may be commenced by the Commission or by any interested person or group filing a petition with the Commission Secretary.

In connection with rule-making proceedings the Commission may conduct investigations, make studies, and hold conferences.

General notice of any proposed rule-making is published in the *Federal Register*. Interested persons or groups may express their views or suggest amendments, revisions, and additions at an oral hearing, if held, or through written statements.

The Commission adopts a rule or order only after consideration of all relevant facts, law, policy, and discretion, including matters presented by interested persons. When adopted, the rule is published in the *Federal Register* to become effective 30 days later.

Industry Guides

The FTC issues administrative interpretations of the textile and fur laws for the guidance of industry in conducting its affairs in conformity with legal requirements. These *industry guides* provide the basis for voluntary and simultaneous abandonment of unlawful practices by industry.

The industry guides may be promulgated by the Commission either on its own initiative or by any interested person or group, when the industry guide would be in the public interest and would serve to bring about more widespread and equitable observance of laws administered by the Commission.

As with the trade regulation rules, the Commission may conduct investigations, make studies, and hold conferences or hearings.

Condemnation Proceedings

In cases arising under the wool and fur acts when it appears that the public interest so requires, the Commission has authority to apply to the courts for condemnation of the products under question.

Injunction Proceedings

In cases arising under the wool, fur, and textile acts, the Commission may apply to the courts for injunctive relief against unlawful sale of products when the Commission deems it to be in the public interest to do so.

For More Information

U.S. Code, Volume 3, 1964 and subsequent supplements provide complete texts of legislation. Available from U.S. Government Printing Office, Washington, D.C.

Rules and regulations issued under the textile acts are available from the Federal Trade Commission, Washington, D.C.

Appendix

Apart from the actual manufacture of textiles and textile products, textile-related activities range from the test-tube to the printed word. The addresses listed in this Appendix suggest the variety of organizations concerned with textiles in the United States.

Manufacturers or Sources

The manufacturers or sources of fibers, fabrics, finishes, and products mentioned in the Textile Handbook are listed below. The reader is reminded that this is a list of sources of products and not necessarily of educational materials.

Abbott Laboratories, Abbott Park, North Chicago, Illinois 60064

Allied Chemical Corporation, Park Avenue and Columbia Road, Morristown, New Jersey 07960

Alrac Corporation, 649 Hope Street, Stamford, Connecticut 06907

American Cyanamid Company, Fibers Division, Wayne, New Jersey 07470

American Enka Corporation, Enka, North Carolina 28728

American Thread Company, High Ridge Park, Stamford, Connecticut 06905

American Velcro, Inc., 406 Brown Avenue, Manchester, New Hampshire 03103

Apex Chemical Company, Inc., 200 South First Street, Elizabethport, New Jersey 07206

Arkansas Company, Inc., P.O. Box 210, Newark, New Jersey 07101

Armo Company, Division of Crown Textile Manufacturing Corporation, 206 West 40th Street, New York, New York 10018

Armour-Dial, Inc., 111 West Clarendon Avenue, Phoenix, Arizona 85077

Avondale Mills, Avondale Avenue, Sylacauga, Alabama 35150

B.T.B. Corporation, 230 Park Avenue, New York, New York 10017

Joseph Bancroft & Sons Company, Rockford Road, Wilmington, Delaware 19899

Bates Fabrics, Inc., 1431 Broadway, New York, New York 10018

Beatrice Foods, 120 South LaSalle Street, Chicago, Illinois 60603

Beaunit Fibers Division of Beaunit Corporation, 261 Madison Avenue, New York, New York 10016

Belding Corticelli, 1430 Broadway, New York, New York 10018

Bendix Corporation, 20650 Civic Center Drive, Southfield, Michigan 48075

Berlou Manufacturing Company, 421 Leader, Marion, Ohio 43302

Best Foods Division, CPC International, International Plaza, Englewood Cliffs, New Jersey 07632

Blackwelder Textile Company, Inc., 314 South Pink Street, Cherryville, North Carolina 28021

Boyle-Midway, 685 Third Avenue, New York, New York 10017

Bradford Dyeing Association, Inc., Main Street, Westerly, Rhode Island 02891

Burlington Industries, Inc., 3330 West Friendly Avenue, Greensboro, North Carolina 27410

Calgon Corporation, Calgon Center, Pittsburgh, Pennsylvania 15230

Carbona Products Company, 30-50 Greenpoint Avenue, Long Island City, New York 11101

Carborundum Company, Carborundum Center, Niagara Falls, New York 14302

Carr-Fulflex, Inc., 92 Franklin, Bristol, Rhode Island 02809

Celanese Corporation, Celanese Fibers Marketing Company, 1211 Avenue of the Americas, New York 10036

Chemicals, Inc., Haverhill, Massachusetts 01830

Chicopee Mills, Inc., 1450 Broadway, New York, New York 10018

Manufacturers or Sources (Continued)

CIBA Chemical & Dye Company, Fair Lawn, New Jersey 07410

Climalene Company, The, 1022 9th Street SW, Canton, Ohio 44707

Clorox Company, The, 7901 Oakport Street, Oakland, California 94623

H. A. Cole Products Company, P. O. Box 9937, Jackson, Mississippi 39206

Colgate-Palmolive Company, 300 Park Avenue, New York, New York 10022

Compax Corporation, 33-35 54th, Woodside, New York 10077

Cone Mills Corporation, 1201 Maple Street, Greensboro, North Carolina 27405

Courtaulds North America, Inc., Highway 43, Mobile, Alabama 36601

CPC International, International Plaza, Englewood Cliffs, New Jersey 07632

Cranston Print Works Company, Worcester Road, Webster, Massachusetts 01570

Cravanette Company, U.S.A., 12 Dudley Street, Providence, Rhode Island 02901

Dan River, Inc., McAlister Plaza, Greenville, South Carolina 29606

Dawbarn Division, W. R. Grace & Company, P. O. Box 460, Waynesboro, Virginia 22980

d-Con Company, Inc., The, Subsidiary of Sterling Drug Co., Inc., 90 Park Avenue, New York, New York 10016

Deering Milliken, Inc., 1045 Avenue of the Americas, New York, New York 10018

Dow Badische Company, Williamsburg, Virginia 23185

Dow Chemical Company, The, Dow Center, Midland, Michigan 48640

Dow Corning Corporation, South Saginaw Road, Midland, Michigan 48641

E. I. du Pont de Nemours & Company, Inc., 1007 Market Street, Wilmington, Delaware 19898

Eastman Chemical Products, Inc., 200 South Wilcox Drive, Kingsport, Tennessee 37662

Enjay Fibers and Laminates Company, Division of Enjay Chemical Company, Odenton, Maryland 21113

FMC Corporation, 111 East Wacker Drive, Chicago, Illinois 60601

Faultless Starch Company, 1025 West 8th Street, Kansas City, Missouri 64101

Ferro Corporation, One Erieview Plaza, Cleveland, Ohio 44114

Fiber Industries, Inc., Highway 70, West Salisbury, North Carolina 28144

Firestone Synthetic Fibers Company, Box 450, Hopewell, Virginia 23860

Fumol Corporation, 49-65 Van Dam Street, Long Island City, New York 11101

General Foods Corporation, 250 North Street, White Plains, New York 10602

Globe Manufacturing Company, 456 Bedford Street, Fall River, Massachusetts 02722

Gold Seal Company, 210 Fourth Street, Bismarck, North Dakota 58501

Greenbelt Consumer Services, 8547 Piney Branch Road, Silver Spring, Maryland 20901

Heberlein Patent Corporation, 350 Fifth Avenue, New York, New York 10001

Herbert Manufacturing Company, Inc., Textile Finishing Department, 505 Eighth Avenue, New York, New York 10018

Hercules Incorporated, 9th and Market Streets, Wilmington, Delaware 19899

Hilex Company, 319 East Kellogg Boulevard, St. Paul, Minnesota 55101

William Hollins & Company, Inc., 666 Fifth Avenue, New York, New York 10036

Hooker Chemical Corporation, 1515 Summer Street, Stamford, Connecticut 06905

Hynson, Westcott & Dunning, Incorporated, Charles and Chase, Baltimore, Maryland 21201

IRC Fibers Division, Midland-Ross Corporation, P. O. Box 580, Painesville, Ohio 44077

Johnson Chemical Company, Inc., 231 Johnson Avenue, Brooklyn, New York 11206

Johnson & Johnson, 501 George, New Brunswick, New Jersey 08903

Jones Chemicals, Inc., 4151 Sunny Sol Boulevard, Caledonia, New York 14423

Koratron Company, Inc., 617 Mission Street, San Francisco, California 94105

Manufacturers or Sources (Continued)

Koret of California, Inc., 617 Mission Street, San Francisco, California 94105

T. B. Lee Company, Inc., 90 Park Avenue, New York, New York 10018

Leesona Corporation, 333 Strawberry Field Road, Warwick, Rhode Island 02886

Lever Brothers Company, 390 Park Avenue, New York, New York 10022

Eli Lilly and Company, 307 East McCarty St., Indianapolis, Indiana 46206

Linco Distributing Corporation, 3631 South Ashland Avenue, Chicago, Illinois 60609

M. Lowenstein & Sons, Inc., 1430 Broadway, New York, New York 10018

Mangels, Herold Company, Inc., Key Highway and Boyle, Baltimore, Maryland 21230

Clarence L. Meyers and Company, Inc., 230 Fairhill Street, Willow Grove, Pennsylvania 19090

Minnesota Mining and Manufacturing Co., 3M Center, St. Paul, Minnesota 55101

Monsanto Company, Textiles Division, 800 N. Lindbergh Boulevard, St. Louis, Missouri 63166

Oakite Products, Inc., 50 Valley Road, Berkeley Heights, New Jersey 07922

Owens-Corning Fiberglas Corporation, Fiberglas Tower, Toledo, Ohio 43601

J. C. Penney, 1301 Avenue of the Americas, New York, New York 10019

Pepperell Manufacturing Company, corner Fourth Avenue and Tenth Street, Westpoint, Georgia 31833

Phillips Fibers Corporation, Subsidiary of Phillips Petroleum Company, P. O. Box 66, Greenville, South Carolina 29602

Playtime Products, Inc., 442 North Detroit Street, Warsaw, Indiana 46580

PPG Industries, Inc., Fiber Glass Division, One Gateway Center, Pittsburgh, Pennsylvania 15222

Procter & Gamble Company, 301 East Sixth Street, Cincinnati, Ohio 45201

Purex Corporation, Ltd., 5101 Clark Avenue, Lakewood, California 90712

Reeves Brothers, Inc., 1271 Avenue of the Americas, New York, New York 10020

Renuzit Home Products Company, 3018 Market Street, Philadelphia, Pennsylvania 19104

Rohm and Haas Company, Independence Mall West, Philadelphia, Pennsylvania 19105

Roman Cleanser Company, 2700 East McNichols Road, Detroit, Michigan 48212

Sage Laboratories, Inc., 3 Huron Drive, Natick, Massachusetts 01760

Sanforized Company, Division of Cluett, Peabody & Co., Inc., 510 Fifth Avenue, New York, New York 10036

Sanitized Sales Company of America, Inc., 200 Madison Avenue, New York, New York 10016

Scott Paper Company, Scott Plaza, Philadelphia, Pennsylvania 19113

Sears, Roebuck and Company, 925 South Homan Avenue, Chicago, Illinois 60607

Shell Chemical Company, One Shell Plaza, Houston, Texas 77001

Southern Lus-Trus Corporation, P. O. Box 9244, Jacksonville, Florida 32208

Spunize Company of America, Inc., 45 South Main Street, Unionville, Connecticut 06085

Stacy Fabrics Corporation, 469 Seventh Avenue, New York, New York 10018

A. E. Staley Manufacturing Company, 2200 East Eldorado Street, Decatur, Illinois 62521

Standard Household Products Corporation, 51 Garfield, Holyoke, Massachusetts 01040

Sterwin Chemicals, Inc., 90 Park Avenue, New York, New York 10016

J. P. Stevens & Co., Inc., 1185 Avenue of the Americas, New York, New York 10036

Stevens Dyers, Ltd. (U.S.A.), 1006 Charles Street, North Providence, Rhode Island 02908

Sunlight Chemical Corp., 55 Pawtucket Avenue, Rumford, Rhode Island 02916

3M Company, 3M Center, St. Paul, Minnesota 55101

Tidy House Products Company, 750 Omaha National Bank Building, Omaha, Nebraska 68001

UniRoyal, Inc., 1230 Avenue of the Americas, New York, New York 10021

Manufacturers or Sources (Continued)

Union Carbide Corporation, Fibers and Fabrics Division, 270 Park Avenue, New York, New York 10017

United Piece Dye Works, Lake Drive, Twin Rivers, Hightstown, New Jersey 08520

White-King, Inc., Terminal Annex, P.O. Box 2198, Los Angeles, California 90051

Trade Associations

Members of trade associations are firms or individuals, usually representing a specific business field. The associations conduct activities to assist their members, to improve the particular area they represent, and to assist the public. Many of them publish educational materials related to their field of interest and may furnish them to educators upon request. Some trade associations in the textiles and related fields include the following:

American Apparel Manufacturers Association, 1611 North Kent Street, Arlington, Virginia 22209

American Carpet Institute (now Carpet and Rug Institute; see below)

American Institute of Laundering (now International Fabricare Institute; see below)

American Institute of Men's and Boys' Wear (now Men's Fashion Association of America; see below)

American Knit Glove Association, Inc. (now National Association of Glove Manufacturers; see below)

American Silk Council, Inc., 299 Madison Avenue, New York, New York 10017

American Textile Manufacturers' Institute, Inc., 1501 Johnston Building, Charlotte, North Carolina 28202

Association of Home Appliance Manufacturers, 20 North Wacker Drive, Chicago, Illinois 60606

Association of Knitted Fabrics Manufacturers, 1450 Broadway, New York, New York 10018

Belgian Linen Association, 280 Madison Avenue, New York, New York 10016

Canvas Products Association International, 600 Endicott Building, St. Paul, Minnesota 55101

Carpet and Rug Institute, P. O. Box 2048, Dalton, Georgia 30720

Chemical Fabrics and Film Association, 60 East 42nd Street, New York, New York 10017

Color Association of the United States, Inc., 200 Madison Avenue, New York, New York 10016

Corduroy Council of America, 527 Madison Avenue, New York, New York 10022

Cotton, Inc., 1370 Avenue of the Americas, New York, New York 10019

Denim Council, 1457 Broadway, Suite 510, New York, New York 10017

Durene Association of America, 350 Fifth Avenue, New York, New York 10001

Fabric Laminators Association, 110 West 40th Street, New York, New York 10018

International Fabricare Institute (headquarters), Doris and Chicago Avenues, Joliet, Illinois 60431

International Fabricare Institute, 8021 Georgia Avenue, Silver Spring, Maryland 20910

International Silk Association (U.S.A.), Inc., 299 Madison Avenue, New York, New York 10017

Knitted Fabrics Institute, Inc., 1450 Broadway, New York, New York 10018

Knitted Outerwear Manufacturers Association, 350 Fifth Avenue, Room 4920, New York, New York 10001

Lace & Embroidery Association of America, Inc. (now Lace Importers Association; see below)

Lace Importers Association, 420 Lexington Avenue, New York, New York 10017

Leavers Lace Manufacturers of America, 1112 Union Trust Building, Providence, Rhode Island 02903

Man-Made Fiber Producers Association, 1150 17th Street NW, Washington, D.C. 20036

Men's Fashion Association of America, 1290 Avenue of the Americas, New York, New York 10019

Narrow Fabrics Institute, Inc., Room 618, 271 North Avenue, New Rochelle, New York 10801

National Association of Glove Manufacturers, 52 South Main Street, Gloversville, New York 12078

National Association of Hosiery Manufacturers, 516 Charlottetown Mall, Charlotte, North Carolina 28204

National Association of Manufacturers, 277 Park Avenue, New York, New York 10017

National Cotton Council of America, 1918 North Parkway, Memphis, Tennessee 38112

National Institute of Drycleaning (now International Fabricare Institute; see above)

National Knitwear Manufacturers Association, 350 Fifth Avenue, Room 4920, New York, New York 10001

National Retail Merchants Association, 100 W. 31st Street, New York, New York 10001

Silk & Rayon Manufacturers Association, 608 Fabian Building, Paterson, New Jersey 07505

Society of the Plastics Industry, Inc., The, 250 Park Avenue, New York, New York 10017

Supima Association of America, 603 First National Building, El Paso, Texas 79901

TIPS (Textile Industry Product Safety), 1750 Pennsylvania Avenue NW, Washington, D.C. 20006

Underwear Institute (now National Knitwear Manufacturers Association; see above)

Vinyl Fabric Institute (now Chemical Fabrics and Film Association; see above)

Wool Bureau, 360 Lexington Avenue, New York, New York 10017

Government Agencies

Several divisions or bureaus within a single government agency may deal with textiles. Information offices of the various agencies and the Government Printing Office supply lists of available publications.

Agricultural Experiment Stations. Located at state land-grant colleges and universities.

Federal Trade Commission, Washington, D.C. 20580

General Services Administration, Washington, D.C. 20405

Government Printing Office, Washington, D.C. 20401

U. S. Department of Agriculture, Washington, D.C. 20250

Regional Offices:

1. Southern Utilization Research & Development Division, Agricultural Research Service, U.S.D.A., P.O. Box 53326, New Orleans, Louisiana 70153 (Conducts extensive research on cotton textiles)

2. Western Utilization Research & Development Division, Agricultural Research Service, U.S.D.A., 2850 Telegraph Avenue, Berkeley, California 94705 (Conducts extensive research on wool textiles)

U. S. Department of Commerce, Washington, D.C. 20230

U. S. Department of Defense, Washington, D.C. 20301

U. S. Naval Supply Depot, Philadelphia, Pennsylvania 19120

U. S. Patent Office, Washington, D.C. 20231

Professional and Scientific Organizations

Professional and scientific organizations conduct programs to advance their areas of interest and serve as clearing houses for new information. Many publish periodicals and technical materials, some of which may be found in local libraries. Among these professional and scientific organizations are the following:

American Association of Textile Chemists and Colorists, P.O. Box 12215, Research Triangle, Durham, North Carolina 27709

American Association for Textile Technology, 295 Fifth Avenue, New York, New York 10016

American Home Economics Association, 2010 Massachusetts Avenue NW, Washington, D.C. 20036

American National Standards Institute, Inc., 1430 Broadway, New York, New York 10018

American Society for Testing and Materials, 1916 Race Street, Philadelphia, Pennsylvania 19103

Institute of Textile Technology, Charlottesville, Virginia 22902

Textile Research Institute, P.O. Box 625, Princeton, New Jersey 08540

Bibliography

This section contains titles of books and periodicals used as references for this fifth edition of the *Textile Handbook*. With perhaps a few exceptions, the books given here are still available according to Bowker's *Books In Print, 1973*. In addition to these resources, the committee for the revision drew information from communications with companies, trade associations, and other sources concerned with textiles or the textile industry. Although many of the resources listed in earlier editions may have furnished unchanging basic material, space does not permit a larger listing to include books no longer in print.

American Fabrics Encyclopedia of Textiles, 2nd ed. Englewood Cliffs, New Jersey: Prentice-Hall, 1972.

ASTM Standards, Part 24, *Textile Materials*. Philadelphia: American Society for Testing and Materials (published annually).

ASTM Standards, Part 25, *Textile Materials*. Philadelphia: American Society for Testing and Materials (published annually).

BACKER, S., *Thesaurus of Textile Terms Covering Fibrous Materials and Processes*, 2nd ed. Cambridge, Massachusetts: M.I.T. Press, 1969.

BIRRELL, V. L., *The Textile Arts: A Handbook of Fabric Structure & Design Processes*. New York: Harper & Row, 1959.

CARTER, M. E., *Essential Fiber Chemistry*. New York: Marcel Dekker, Inc., 1971.

CLARKE, W., *Introduction to Textile Printing*, 3rd ed. Plainfield, New Jersey: Textile Book Service, 1971.

COCKETT, S. R., and K. A. HILTON, *Dyeing of Cellulosic Fibres and Related Processes*. New York: Academic Press, Inc., 1961.

COLLIER, A. M., *A Handbook of Textiles*. Elmsford, New York: Pergamon Press, Inc., 1971.

COOK, J. G., *Handbook of Polyolefin Fibres*. Watford, England: Merrow Publishing Company, 1967.

COOK, J. G., *Handbook of Textile Fibres*, 2 Vols., 4th ed. Watford, England: Merrow Publishing Company, 1968.

Cotton from Field to Fabric, 5th ed. Memphis, Tennessee: National Cotton Council, 1951.

COWAN, M. L., and M. E. JUNGERMAN, *Introduction to Textiles*, 2nd ed. New York: Appleton-Century-Crofts, 1969.

DEMBECK, A. A., *Guidebook to Man-Made Textile Fibers & Textured Yarns of the World*, 3rd ed. New York: United Piece Dye Works, 1969.

DENNY, G. G., *Fabrics*, 8th ed. Philadelphia: J. B. Lippincott Company, 1962.

GARNER, W., *Textile Laboratory Manual*, 6 Vols., 3rd ed. London: National Trade Press, 1967.

GROVER, E. B., and D. S. HAMBY, *Handbook of Textile Testing and Quality Control*. Plainfield, New Jersey: Textile Book Service, 1960.

HAEFELE, C. L., R. C. DAVIS, F. FORTESS, R. T. HUNTER, and W. A. ST. JOHN, *The Technology of Home Laundering*. Monograph No. 108. New York: American Association for Textile Technology, Inc., 1973.

HALL, A. J., *Textile Finishing*, 3rd ed. New York: American Elsevier, 1966.

HAMBY, D. S. (ed.). *American Cotton Handbook*, 2 Vols., 3rd ed. New York: John Wiley & Sons, Inc., 1965.

HATHORNE, B. L., *Woven Stretch and Textured Fabrics*. New York: John Wiley & Sons, Inc., 1964.

HEARLE, J. W., *Structural Mechanics of Fibers, Yarns, & Fabrics*, Vol. 1. Plainfield, New Jersey: Textile Book Service, 1969.

HOLLEN, N., and J. SADDLER, *Textiles*, 4th ed. New York: The Macmillan Company, 1973.

JOSEPH, M. L., and A. GIESEKING, *Illustrated Guide to Textiles*, 2nd ed. Fullerton, California: Plycon Press, 1972.

JOSEPH, M. L., *Introductory Textile Science*, 2nd ed. New York: Holt, Rhinehart & Winston, Inc., 1972.

KASWELL, E. R., *Handbook of Industrial Textile* (Edited by Wellington Sears). Plainfield, New Jersey: Textile Book Service, 1963.

KLAPPER, M., *Fabric Almanac*, 2nd ed. New York: Fairchild Publications, Inc., 1971.

KLAPPER, M., *Textile Glossary*. New York: Fairchild Publications, Inc., 1973.

KORNER, R., *Technical Dictionary of Textile Finishing*. Elmsford, New York: Pergamon Press, Inc., 1967. (English, French, German, Russian.)

KORNREICH, E., *Introduction to Fibres and Fabrics*, 2nd ed. New York: American Elsevier Publishing Company, Inc., 1966.

LANCASHIRE, J. B., *Jacquard Design and Knitting*. Plainfield, New Jersey: Textile Book Service, 1969.

LINTON, G. E., *Applied Basic Textiles*. Plainfield, New Jersey: Textile Book Service, 1973.

LINTON, G. E., *Modern Textile & Apparel Dictionary*. Plainfield, New Jersey: Textile Book Service, 1973.

LINTON, G. E., *Natural and Manmade Textile Fibers*. Plainfield, New Jersey: Textile Book Service, 1966.

LINTON, G. E., and H. COHEN, *Chemistry and Textiles for the Laundry Industry*. Plainfield, New Jersey: Textile Book Service, 1961.

LYNN, J. E., and J. J. PRESS, *Advances in Textile Processing*. Huntington, New York: R. E. Krieger Publishing Company, 1961.

LYONS, J. W., *Chemistry and Uses of Fire Retardants*. New York: Wiley-Interscience, 1970.

McDONALD, M., *Nonwoven Fabric Technology*. Park Ridge, New Jersey: Noyes Data Corp., 1971.

Man-Made Fiber Fact Book. Washington, D.C.: Man-Made Fiber Producers Association, Inc., 1972.

MARK, H. F., *et al.* (eds.), *Encyclopedia of Polymer Science and Technology*, 15 Vols. New York: Wiley-Interscience, 1964-1971.

MARK, H. F., S. M. ATLAS, and E. CERNIA, *Man-Made Fibers*, 3 Vols. Plainfield, New Jersey: Textile Book Service, 1968.

MARSH, J. T., *Introduction to Textile Finishing*, 2nd ed. New York: Barnes & Noble, 1966.

MONCRIEFF, R. W., *Man-Made Fibers*, 5th ed. New York: John Wiley & Sons, Inc., 1963.

MORTON, W. E., and J. W. S. HEARLE, *Physical Properties of Textile Fibers*. London: Butterworth & Co., 1962.

PETERS, R. H., *Textile Chemistry*, Vol. I. Plainfield, New Jersey: Textile Book Service, 1963.

PETERS, R. H., *Textile Chemistry*, Vol. II. Plainfield, New Jersey: Textile Book Service, 1967.

PIZZUTO, J. J., *One Hundred-One Weaves in One Hundred-One Fabrics*. Plainfield, New Jersey: Textile Book Service, 1961.

POTTER, M. D., and B. P. CORBMAN, *Textiles: Fiber to Fabric*, 4th ed. New York: McGraw-Hill Book Company, 1967.

REICHMAN, C., *Knitting Dictionary*. Plainfield, New Jersey: Textile Book Service, 1966.

REICHMAN, C., (ed. in chief), *Knitting Encyclopedia*. Plainfield, New Jersey: Textile Book Service, 1972.

REICHMAN, C., *Knitted Stretch Technology*. Plainfield, New Jersey: Textile Book Service, 1965.

REICHMAN, C., *et al.*, *Knitted Fabric Primer*. Plainfield, New Jersey: Textile Book Service, 1967.

REISFELD, A., *Warp Knit Engineering*. Plainfield, New Jersey: Textile Book Service, 1966.

SKINKLE, J. H., *Textile Testing: Physical, Chemical & Microscopical*, 2nd ed. Plainfield, New Jersey: Textile Book Service, 1949.

STOUT, E. E., *Introduction to Textiles*, 3rd ed. New York: John Wiley & Sons, Inc., 1970.

Textile Fibers and Their Properties. Greensboro, North Carolina: Burlington Industries, 1970.

Textile Finishing Glossary, 4th ed. Greensboro, North Carolina: Cone Mills Corporation, 1967.

Von Bergen, W., *Wool Handbook*, Vol. I, 3rd ed. New York: John Wiley & Sons, Inc., 1970.

Von Bergen, W., *Wool Handbook*, Vol. II, Part 2, 3rd ed. New York: John Wiley & Sons, Inc., 1970.

Whittaker, C. M., and C. C. Wilcock, *Dyeing with Coal-Tar Dyestuffs*, 5th ed. London: Bailliere, Tindall and Cox, 1964.

Ward, D. T., *Tufting: An Introduction*. London: Textile Business Press, 1969.

Weaver, J. W. (ed.), *Analytical Methods for a Textile Laboratory*. Research Triangle Park, North Carolina: American Association of Textile Chemists and Colorists, 1968.

Wingate, I. (ed.), *Fairchild's Dictionary of Textiles*. New York: Fairchild Publications, Inc., 1967.

Wingate, I., *Textile Fabrics & Their Selection*, 6th ed. Englewood Cliffs, New Jersey: Prentice-Hall, Inc., 1970.

Periodicals

American Dyestuff Reporter, SAF International Inc., 44 East 23rd Street, New York, New York 10010

American Fabrics, Doric Publishing Co., Inc., 24 East 38th Street, New York, New York 10016

America's Textile Reporter, Bennett Enterprises, Inc., Daniel Bldg., Greenville, South Carolina 29602

CIBA Review, CIBA, Ltd., Klybeckstr, 141, 4000 Basel, Switzerland

Daily News Record, Fairchild Publications, Inc., 7 East 12th Street, New York, New York 10003

Home Furnishings Daily, Fairchild Publications, Inc., 7 East 12th Street, New York, New York 10003

Journal of the Textile Institute, Textile Institute, 10 Blackfriars Street, Manchester 3, England

Modern Knitting Management, Rayon Publishing Corp., 303 Fifth Avenue, New York, New York 10016

Modern Textiles Magazine, Rayon Publishing Corp., 303 Fifth Avenue, New York, New York 10016

Textile Bulletin, Clark Publishing Co., 302 W. Morehead Street, Charlotte, North Carolina 28202

Textile Chemist and Colorist, AATCC, P.O. Box 12215, Research Triangle Park, Durham, North Carolina 27709

Textile Industries, W. R. C. Smith Publishing Co., 1760 Peachtree Rd., N.W., Atlanta, Georgia 30309

Textile Month, Textile Business Press, 300 East 42nd Street, New York, New York 10017

Textile Organon, Textile Economics Bureau, Inc., 10 East 40th Street, New York, New York 10016

Textile Research Journal, Textile Research Institute, Box 625, Princeton, New Jersey 08540

Textile World, McGraw-Hill Book Company, 330 West 42nd Street, New York, New York 10036

Women's Wear Daily, Fairchild Publications, Inc., 7 East 12th Street, New York, New York 10003

Index

DATE DUE

GAYLORD			PRINTED IN U.S.A.